No More
Front Porches

Rebuilding Community
in Our Isolated Worlds

LINDA   WILCOX

Beacon Hill Press of Kansas City
Kansas City, Missouri

Library of Congress Cataloging-in-Publication Data

Wilcox, Linda, 1950—
    No more front porches : rebuilding community in our isolated worlds / Linda Wilcox.
        p. cm.
    Includes bibliographical references.
    ISBN 0-8341-1886-6 (pbk.)
        1. Community. 2. Community life—United States. 3. Social isolation—United States. I. Title.

HM756 .W55 2002
306.7—dc21

2001052878

10 9 8 7 6 5 4 3 2 1

To Jim, Josh, Ben, Lori, and Ethan—
my favorite front-porch people

Contents

Acknowledgments

Ironically, this book about community, like most books, was written in isolation. I often went to my office early in the morning or late at night and cloistered myself in order to get it completed. But though it was written alone, it was not accomplished without the valued advice and experienced criticism of many trusted advisors.

My husband, Jim, a true wordsmith and accomplished author, provided many hours of editing and many more hours of encouragement. Not since I wrote my dissertation 10 years ago have I depended on him more for his invaluable knowledge of rhetoric and grammar. His background in journalistic writing helped me stay on course.

There are eight others to whom I am extremely grateful for their inspiration and kindly criticism. I thank Jon Johnson, Jerry Hull, Carolyn Morgan, and Wil Scott for inspiring me to teach and to do research in sociology. I thank good friends Sheryl Lidzy, Bonnie Sanders, Kathy Williams, and Dennis Williams for their help in making this book come alive.

I am indebted to the community of students, faculty, and staff at Southern Nazarene University who allowed me the necessary time and space over many months to complete the research and writing. They have taught me much about life in community. And finally, I thank the members of the editorial staff at Beacon Hill Press of Kansas City who came up with the title for the book and who have believed all along in the value of this project.

PART 1

Communities
That Isolate Us

If we want to rebuild community,
we must understand the communities that isolate us.

As we look at our families, neighborhoods, and churches today, it's easy to see hindrances to living in the old-fashioned "front-porch" communities of the past.

What is it about our modern culture that seems to discourage our taking time to slow down and enjoy life instead of racing through it? What in our demanding lives prevents us from spending time with our families, from getting to know our neighbors and the people with whom we worship?

Sometimes we don't even seem to have time to connect with the people with whom we live, let alone everyone else. How did our lives become so busy? What can we do to build genuine community when our society seems to be determined to isolate us? Our first task is to take a look at just where we are—in our families, neighborhoods, and churches—and examine how we got here. The loss of community didn't just happen. What caused it, and, most important, how can we fix it?

Like it or not, given the rapid social changes of the last half-century, our communities may never again look like those of the 1950s. With our high divorce rate, many adults and children live in blended families, with all the complications these arrangements bring. In families in which both parents work outside the home, no one may be at home during the day to build relationships with neighbors.

And with our highly mobile society, we may hesitate to get to know families in the church, because they could be gone next month when their work transfers them across the country.

All of this makes us wonder if we'll ever put down roots anywhere, because you never know what the future holds. As a result, many people hop from church to church and never join a local congregation, much less become loyal to a particular denomination. And when we do find a church we like, we often don't want any demands made on us. We just want to sit in a nice padded pew, listen to great music, and be "spiritually fed" each week. In other words, we want a "me-first" church.

But if we're serious in our desire for genuine community, how can we make it a reality in our lives? Do we need to know some things about where we've come from, how our world has changed, and how it's likely to continue to change?

What are the answers, and where do we sign up to change our communities for the better?

In Part 1 we will look at how our families, neighbor-hoods, and churches have changed and why. We will note how our society has evolved over the years and examine the changes that often result in *communities that isolate us.* Our busy, modern lives seem to leave little room for community building, but in spite of this, many of us are finding ways to stay connected, and some of us are discovering that our front porches haven't totally disappeared, that they've just taken on new forms—out of necessity.

1

No More Front Porches

*The sun was gone, but he had left his footprints
in the sky. It was the time for sitting on porches.*
—Zora Neale Hurston
in *Their Eyes Were Watching God*

*Let love and faithfulness never leave you;
bind them around your neck, write them
on the tablet of your heart. Then you will win favor
and a good name in the sight of God and man.*
—Prov. 3:3-4

Whatever happened to those big front porches that
every house once had—the ones we used to sit on
for hours with family and friends, sipping iced tea and
catching up on everybody's news?

**It's possible to lead separate lives from the very people
who in the past would have been closest to us.**

Where are those old-fashioned neighborhoods where
everybody looked out for each other, especially the kids?

What happened to the little community churches where
people knew the names of every person and welcomed each
other with a big pat on the back, a hug, and "Well, it's so
good to see you, Brother Baker"?

Whatever happened to the sense of belonging we felt as we looked at these people on their porches, in our neighborhoods, or at our churches, people who meant more to us than anything in the world?

Before we get completely carried away on this nostalgic road trip, we probably should look back and see if these "front porch societies" were truly as we remember them. Were they really so idyllic, so perfect? We may also want to reconsider this sense of loss and see if perhaps some modern versions of these societies persist today. And finally, we should explore ways we can glean the good from the old-fashioned communities and create a new formula that will work for us now.

Doubtless the demands of modern life can leave us feeling isolated. We need only to look at advances in personal technology within the last decade to get an idea of the emphasis on individualism in our society. It's possible to isolate ourselves from our family, friends, and neighbors all in the name of progress. It's possible to lead separate lives from the very people who in the past would have been closest to us.

Given the easy access to the Internet, we can also carry on "cyber relationships" with strangers on the other side of the world, sometimes to the exclusion of face-to-face interaction. Counselors, clergy, and marriage therapists used to hear, "He's not communicating with me." Now it's more often replaced with "He's communicating with the computer and not me."

How can we welcome the numerous conveniences and advantages of the new technology without sacrificing human contact and interaction?

Recently two other professors and I took a group of college students and community people on a trip through the South as the culmination of a class we had taught on Southern literature and culture. It was a fabulous introduction to the language, foods, lifestyles, histories, and literature of that unique culture.

As we traveled through Tennessee, Mississippi, and Louisiana, we were struck by the architecture of these areas, in many ways vastly different from where I grew up farther north and where I live now in the Midwest.

All during the trip, we saw lovely houses with little porches that included a couple of chairs and a few plants; magnificent estates with wide, sweeping verandas wrapping around the entire front of the structure, some hung with lush green ferns and electric fans overhead. Some of these porches could seat 20 people or more, while others were small enough to be called "stoops" in the North. Some porches were more like greenhouses, with scores of plants; others, with all their animals out front, could have been considered kennels. We also saw porches where parties were in full swing until the wee hours of the morning.

We also saw what my dad would have called "hang dawg" porches that were barely held together with bailing wire and good wishes. And we saw that staple of front porches, the bare-boarded ones with old couches and car seats that had been stashed there "temporarily" six years ago.

All of these can be found throughout the United States, but we were amazed at the number we saw on this trip: porches being used by people actually sitting on them, talking, and visiting with their neighbors.

Front porches, unlike back porches or patios, have the advantage of connecting us with our families and our communities at the same time.

We sat on Marjorie Cartwright's front porch outside Oxford, Mississippi, and waved to the neighbors across the street, also sitting on their front porches. Mrs. Cartwright is the grandmother of one of the professors, and after dinner at her house, all 35 of us thought it just seemed the right thing to do to sit on the front porch and enjoy the summer evening. Without air conditioning in the house, it was much cooler outside anyway. We even learned why the ceilings in the South are commonly painted pale blue: to keep the bugs away.

This trip reminded us of Clarisse in *Fahrenheit 451,* who lamented the loss of the front porches of the past, "No front porches. My uncle says there used to be front porches. And people sat there sometimes at night, talking when they wanted to talk, rocking, and not talking when they didn't want to talk. Sometimes they just sat there and thought about things, turned things over."[1]

Throughout my life I have known and loved many front porches, places where I could sit with my family and observe all that was going on in my community. According to North Carolina historians, front porches are appealing because, unlike back porches or patios, they have the advantage of connecting us with our families *and* our communities at the same time; that's what sets them apart. They are outdoor living areas where we are both public and private.

Probably originating in coastal North Carolina, the porch, gallery, veranda, or piazza was the area of transition from the public to the private. It provided shelter from the elements. The first porches may have been built by African slaves, East Indian immigrants, to adapt to the hot, humid weather. The style of the porches made statements about the owners' level of social prestige: cabins had small porches, while wealthy families often adorned their homes with massive, ornately structured Greek porticos. Today some of the traditional porch rituals of the South still persist in the North Carolina countryside, where homeowners turn their front porch chairs upside down to indicate that they are not receiving visitors.

I remember my grandparents' narrow front porch that ran the length of their big red house in Asbury, West Virginia. It seemed to me that my grandparents knew everyone in their community, for they waved at each passing car. I didn't learn until later that everybody waves to everybody in most rural areas, whether they know each other or not. We often sat out there with all our aunts, uncles, and cousins. When we didn't have enough chairs for everybody, the kids sat wherever they could—usually on adults' laps or on the porch railing. More often than not, we were playing in my grandparents' enormous front yard.

I also remember the older folks' suspicion of any strange car in the neighborhood. "Now, who do you suppose *that* is? And why are they turning into the Gilkersons' driveway?" This observation would be followed by hours of speculation. Eventually somebody got on the local "party line" telephone, and the mystery was solved. Of course, if we waited for a few days, the local paper would actually publish the story that the Gilkersons had had weekend guests visiting from Great Neck, New York. Small town newspapers are always trying to scoop the big story.

Why do we long for the remnants of the past and fantasize that life was really better back then, when its pace seemed so much slower?

When I was a kid, we also spent countless hours waiting on the front porch for the mail to be delivered. In the summertime, while we waited and drank red Kool-Aid, we counted any out-of-state license plates we happened to see on our county road. Having learned from the grownups, we speculated the purpose of these "foreigners" in our community, even if they were just passing through. But eventually they were forgotten when the pick-up mail truck came down our rural route and loaded our metal box with the Sears catalog, the electric bill, and a letter from Aunt Dorothy —all in one day! These are great memories.

What is so appealing about these "front porch communities"? Why do we long for the remnants of the past and fantasize that life was really better back then, when its pace seemed so much slower? And how has modern technology affected our interaction with each other? In what ways are some among us isolated from the group—alone among the many? Have we made room for some and not others? And can we work to rebuild "front porch communities" that work for our modern culture?

It is the purpose of this book to find some answers to these questions. We will look at communities, past and present, to examine how we romanticize cultures of the past, to explore ways our communities have changed, and to devise ways to make our interaction with each other more genuine.

Perhaps most importantly, we will examine what people of faith can do to rebuild strong families, neighborhoods, and church communities. Unfortunately, in the past we Christians have often been among the first to hide from cultural changes around us.

Does this have to be our reaction? Can we be a part of the solution for today's problems if we're hiding out somewhere? Probably not. In this book we explore God's plan for us as communities of fellowship, along with the privileges and responsibilities His plan involves. We will discover what we as Christians can do to rebuild real "front porch" families, neighborhoods, and churches.

For Reflection and Discussion

1. Is it really possible to "build community," or is it something that just happens?

2. Why do you think we seem to be nostalgic about and romanticize the way we think life used to be? What are some of the ways we do this?

3. When your older relatives talk about the "good old days," what do they emphasize?

4. What's so appealing about "front porch communities"?

5. List some ways technology has become a benefit and/or a detriment to community life.

6. The author maintains that in the past Christians have often been among the first to "hide from cultural changes." Do you agree or disagree? What are some examples of hiding?

7. What are some of the "privileges and responsibilities" of living in genuine communities of faith?

2

Our Hyper-Scheduled Lives

*Our lives are connected
by a thousand different threads.*
—Herman Melville

*May the God of hope fill you with all joy and peace
as you trust in him, so that you may overflow
with hope and power.*
—Rom. 15:13

Joanna gets up at 5:00 A.M. and is on the road by 5:30. Two appointments wait before her day officially begins at 8:30. Eating a nutrition bar and trying to keep from dozing off, she rides through the deserted streets in the family van. The rest of her day stretches before her, carefully scripted with assignments, meetings, and special appointments, all written down the night before in her day planner. Hopefully everything will run smoothly today and she'll be everywhere she's supposed to be with all the necessary equipment and on time. Maybe she won't get the cold that the rest of the family has—that would mess up the schedule entirely. With all her commitments, she knows it will again be dark before she returns home this evening.

Joanna sighs, wondering if she's trying to do too much. And what will it be like next year—when she's in the eighth grade?

For many families in the United States this scenario is routine. Weekdays are filled with school, piano lessons, play practice, football games, soccer, tutoring, scout meetings, dance rehearsals, clubs, boards, and church activities—and that's just one child. Multiply this by four, and it's a nightmare just trying to stay on schedule.

For years, families depended on a schedule on the refrigerator door to remind them of events—but for many, that's no longer sufficient. Today many new homes have an office and schedule center built into the kitchen. Here the master schedule is kept with all the weekly events penciled in.

In some cases the family depends on Mom's hand-held computer scheduler to keep them all on track. Numerous on-line family organizers hold a date book, address book, and calendar. One of these, Audrey (from the 3Com Corporation), is touted as the first digital home assistant and is advertised with the slogan "Simple sets you free."

Why we are demanding this kind of involvement or "hyperscheduling" of ourselves and our children?

But whether you're using old refrigerator magnets, the kitchen schedule center, or Audrey, just keeping up with where everyone is supposed to be at every hour is a full-time job. And if someone gets sick or a game time is changed, the whole family schedule must be rearranged. Another full-time job is providing transportation to all these events. The family van can be at only one place at a time, but it needs to be at three. A parent can be at only one place at a time, but his or her presence is required at three.

What's a parent to do? In the movie *Multiplicity*, Michael Keaton creates several copies of himself in order to get everything done. Funny, but probably not realistic for the near future. We probably need to ask, "Why are we demanding this kind of involvement or 'hyperscheduling' of ourselves and our children?"

According to Alvin Rosenfeld and Nicole Wise, authors of *Hyper-Parenting: Are You Hurting Your Child by Trying Too Hard?* one reason we do too much is because we *can*.[1]

Unlike our ancestors, we no longer have to spend our days in hard, physical labor to put food on the table and a roof over the family's head. Today, for most of us, those needs are taken care of, and we can spend our time providing extras for our children.

But are the results always positive? According to recent research focusing on children, by the age of 18, 20 percent have suffered a major depression, and nearly 9 percent of teens have been diagnosed with anxiety disorders.[2] Children are commonly taken for counseling because their parents feel they have little motivation and are not aggressive enough to succeed.

We may also attempt to do too many things at once. We may be teaching our children that something is wrong with relaxing.

Besides having the time to get extras for our families, we are also motivated to prove ourselves as parents and to compare ourselves with other parents. We want to be good parents, and we want to provide for our children, but most of us feel less than adequate for the task. We question our ability to be good parents. There seems to be an epidemic of guilt about parenting and measuring up to the family down the street. Our anxiety and competitive spirits motivate us to attempt to do more than is perhaps healthful for us and for our children.

We may also attempt to do too many things at once. We may be teaching our children that something is wrong with relaxing. We have to be accomplishing something, everything has to have a purpose, and we have to have something to show for our time. Our goal becomes getting as much done in as little time as possible, so we cram several activities into the little time we do have. The daily commute in the family van becomes an experiment in "multitasking." Dad drives while shaving, listening to the news, and making a car repair appointment on his cell phone. Mom is making a list of her client appointments, listening to the market report on her earphones, and calling her son's school about the fundraiser. There's no way they can hear the poetry being recited from the back seat. It's overwhelming.

Our kids pick up the behaviors being modeled. I once came home to find my 17-year-old playing his guitar, listening to two stereos, watching television, and talking on the phone. I fully expected him to say, "I *am* doing my homework!"

Of course we want our children to be involved in school and in after-school activities. We want them to take music lessons and participate in athletics. And who could deny acting lessons to a future star of stage and screen whose fourth-grade teacher assures us she has real potential? Our other child is musically gifted, so we can't deny her the private flute lessons.

We don't want to stunt the growth and stifle the potential of our kids. What kind of parents would we be? Add to this the pressure we feel from other parents in the neighborhood and at church who seem to deny their children nothing. Our kids remind us that we're the only ones home on a Thursday night. Everybody else from school "has a life" and is at the new model plane exhibition field. Where does it all stop? Perhaps a better question is "Where did it all begin?"

A suburban middle school outside Chicago now offers 50 clubs and 90 sports choices to its students. It's not surprising that this school of 1,200 also requires all its students to use day planners. The teachers assure the parents that the children are being taught to organize their days and take responsibility for their commitments. The average student cannot possibly remember all his daily assignments, meetings, and practice schedules, so the planners are essential.

But many wonder if all this activity may be too much. An *NBC Nightly News* segment (October 6, 2000) asked, "Are we too busy for our own good?" According to the report, "busyness" has become a national status symbol with families rushing from event to event and complaining to friends and family about their crowded schedules. "We just have no idea how we'll do all that our schedules demand of us. We're just way too busy."

Sometimes these recitations of family commitments take on an air of self-importance. Complaining about busy schedules begins to sound like bragging about how talented and gifted our children are and how important we are to have been asked to sit on the advisory board or the new parents' group. Where does this need for "busyness" come from? Is anything really wrong with it?

My husband and I have some friends whose children were born about the same time as ours, and we've all watched their four and our two become young adults. We don't see this couple as often now, but when we do, we have the same conversation that we've had for the last 20 years. During the summer when our kids were playing in the backyard sprinkler, theirs were enrolled in three summer camps, scheduled to make two educational trips, and each was in more than one summer sports league. While we were making grilled cheese sandwiches and cherry Kool-Aid lunches, they were rushing from game to game and practice after practice, eating drive-through meals in the car on the way. (Actually our meals weren't all that nutritious either.)

These are good friends of ours—wonderful people and marvelous parents. They care about their kids as much as we care about ours. And it's not a matter of income differences. But when we see them, the conversation always begins with

"We're *so* tired. We had three games last night, the kids leave for another camp tomorrow, and we haven't had a meal together at the dining room table for weeks. We're just too busy! What have *you* been doing?"

Don't we know this is the 21st-century United States, and we're supposed to be joining sports leagues, getting our kids involved, and we should all be tired from running around all day? What's wrong with us?

My husband looks at me, I look at him, and we both sheepishly answer, "Nothing." We hesitantly reveal that we slept late on Saturday, watched cartoons, made waffles for the kids, and then watched them play ping pong with the neighborhood kids in our garage. Later they had a water balloon fight instigated by my husband, who was on the roof, pelting the bigger kids before they knew what had hit them. Later that night we watched "Johnny the Hoppy," the big toad who has lived in our backyard for years (they can live for 35 years, you know), catch june bugs. And that night after everybody got their showers, we all collapsed and read together. We didn't go anywhere all day, and we didn't spend any money. Our friends look at us as if we have snakes coming out of our ears.

Don't we know this is the 21st-century United States, and we're supposed to be joining sports leagues, getting our kids involved, and we should all be tired from running around all day? *What's wrong with us?* They're astonished at our boring life and shake their heads with pity that those poor Wilcox kids never get to do anything.

Another family we know has all the latest technological toys. They love this stuff. Each of their kids has a television set, stereo, and videocassette recorder (VCR) in their rooms. No computer or video game has yet been introduced that this family has not tested, rented, or purchased. They have a new innovation and high-tech appliance or toy at their house every week. They have it all—or at least that's what our kids say when they try to convince us that "There's nothing to do at our house. We want to go over there to play—it's boring here." Of course, this was part of our plan—to establish a home that was so boring that eventually our sons would actually have to use their imaginations and draw on their own creativity to play.

In a *Newsweek* commentary, "We're Too Busy for Ideas," Michele McCormick says when she recently got a portable radio/headphone (she's sure she's one of the last people in North America to get one), she began to realize her "best ideas occur . . . when my mind is otherwise unchallenged and there is no pressure . . . once I was fully plugged in, things stopped occurring to me . . . . That's why unplugged time is vital."[3]

Somewhere along the line my husband and I got the idea that we were supposed to sit and eat together at the end of the day. Something seemed to be sacred about that.

At our house this unplugged time often resulted in huge messes in the backyard or the garage as our boys took apart anything that wasn't hidden and then had too many pieces left over when they attempted to put them back together. Or when they developed detailed plans to tunnel their way underground from their rooms to the backyard—fortunately this plan never got farther then the paper diagram. They were shocked that we didn't see the genius of this idea. Then there was the extremely loud and minimally talented garage band that met at our house all summer one year—my ears are still ringing from that one. I'll have to admit, though, that it was hard sometimes for their books, forts, and lemonade

stands to compete with all the modern technology across
the street. And I also have to admit that at times "keeping up
with the neighbors" was tempting.

It's not that they or we are better parents. That's not the
point. The point is that somewhere along the line my husband and I got the idea that we were supposed to sit and eat
together at the end of the day. Something seemed to be sacred about that. We're not better parents because we tried to
do this, but we were definitely less harried. Yes, our sons par-
ticipated in sports leagues, but only in one league at a time.
Yes, they took music lessons, but only one instrument at a
time. Yes, they were both involved in school activities, but
not many. They did go to church camp, Sunday School, and
youth group events.

But through all of this, we tried to reserve time to be together and to eat together when we could. We made lots of
mistakes as parents, but apparently we got this one right. Little did we know that years later, social and behavioral scientists would discover that children may be physically, emotionally, and psychologically healthier if they eat dinner
together with their family.

How could this one little activity make such a difference? From recent research, we're learning that there just
may be something magical about sitting down together,
looking across the table at each other, and talking over a
meal. These studies found that in families making this a priority, the children seemed to do better when they reached
their teen years.[4] A study of National Merit Scholars found
that one characteristic many winners had in common was
that their families ate dinner together. Whether the meals
were prepared at home or brought in, eating together made
a difference.

In *Child of Mine: Feeding with Love and Good Sense,* Ellyn
Satter maintains that "well-adjusted children are not created
out of thin air. The ritual of eating together as a family that

allows for a positive connection between parents and their children usually starts early on and tends to be a reflection of the concern and respect that mothers and fathers show in all areas of child rearing."[5]

I can't tell you how many times we had fish sticks, macaroni and cheese, and green peas. My family still runs screaming into the streets when I mention this meal. My husband once made tacos, hot dogs, and pancakes for dinner—on the same night! We had spaghetti, casseroles, and the dreaded meatloaf. I once made a hot chicken salad that nobody would taste. So undoubtedly our cooking was *not* so magical.

The conversations around the table were not always stimulating either. There were often uproarious, occasionally intellectually challenging, frequently hilarious, and sometimes uncomfortable discussions as we talked about grades and school behavior. Sometimes we faced food fights and arguments about whose turn it was to do the dishes. And we always endured the challenge to get the kids to eat everything on their plates. A few years ago we found several wedges of dried up apple on a ledge under the table, left there years ago by a wily fourth grader. So the difference is not necessarily what you eat or what you talk about.

The difference seems to be that, when possible, you eat at home together, not looking at the back of somebody's head as you barrel down the road toward the YMCA.

Wishing we could turn back the clock to "the ideal 1950s" only makes us feel worse—especially for families in which both parents have to work—and that's most of us.

Unfortunately, the demands of our modern lives often prevent us from having these family dinners. In most households, both parents work outside the home, and neither has much energy to create a meal at the end of the day. With school and church activities nearly every night of the week, it's hard to get everyone in the same place at the same time and get the food ready when they are.

Many people lament that the "good old days," when mothers stayed at home and prepared dinner for everyone, are gone forever, and they probably are. Wishing we could turn back the clock to "the ideal 1950s" only makes us feel worse—especially for families in which both parents *have* to work—and that's most of us.

What can we do to improve our families' hurried lives? How can we shape our world so dinner together is not just a possibility, but a priority for more of us?

A few years ago I arrived at my church on a Wednesday night and saw several young parents dragging their children into the building, some of the kids having fallen asleep in the car on the way. None of these parents had been home since early that morning—having picked up the children at school, raced to piano lessons and ball practice, picked up dinner on the way, and now they were at church for choir practice, worship, and children's church.

They were all exhausted and looked as if they would love to have a night off. But because they were good church members, because the church held scheduled activities that night, or because it was a "sin" to be anywhere else when the church doors were open, they felt responsible to be there. I wondered if God might be more pleased if everybody just took a nap.

One of the best survival strategies I have encountered is the revolutionary idea of "just saying no." I'm talking about learning to say no even when we're asked to do perfectly legitimate and worthwhile tasks—learning to say, "No, I have other plans," even when those plans are simply to spend time at home with the family. What a liberating idea! You'll be surprised how good this feels and how that job will somehow get done without you.

You don't want to say no to everything. Most churches need volunteers to teach classes, be camp counselors, serve as ushers, and more. But when you're a young parent who's baking cupcakes for 24 fifth-graders, car-pooling with six middle school boys (all who seem to think that more cologne is better), and coaching the church basketball team—it might be OK to say no to filling in for the nursery worker who couldn't make it that night. They'll find someone else.

When people are involved in a life-threatening accident or illness and they survive, they always say, "I'm going to slow down and spend more time with my family." They never say they're going to work harder.

Unfortunately, as the saying goes, 20 percent of the church people do 80 percent of the work. If you're willing to live at the church because you're the one with talent or because you're the one who can't say no, you'll be kept busy volunteering—too busy for family dinners together.

Does this sound like heresy? It does to many people. But if you'll talk to older parents, many will tell you they wish they had spent more time with their families along the way. When people are involved in a life-threatening accident or illness and they survive, they always say, "I'm going to slow down and spend more time with my family." They never say they're going to work harder. They never say they're going to turn their life around and make more money. Instead, they make plans to spend more time with their families.

In recent years, several authors and speakers have focused on simplifying our lives. Scale back on your wants and "needs," and slow down the pace of your life. Cut back on the activities you say yes to and don't confuse "busyness" with importance.

Some of my colleagues in the past were consumed with the idea that to be valuable meant to be busy. They seemed to think that "busy" equals "good." They acted as though unless they were constantly working, they were not good people and not good workers. They often used to tell me about being in their offices from dawn until late in the evening, working. They spent their vacations in their offices, researching and organizing, or they spent vacations dragging their families to professional conferences.

Where do we get this idea that to be valuable means being busy? Of course, we all value hard work. We aren't really slackers, or we wouldn't be able to do our jobs. Also, it's unlikely that we will succeed in our careers without working hard, and we will need to put in the necessary hours to make this happen. Hard work is a core value of our society.

But I'm talking about more than working hard and doing an honest day's work for an honest day's pay. I'm talking about more than volunteering at the church or in the community because it's the right thing to do. I'm talking about linking busy, hectic lives with our value as people and our value as Christians, when Christ teaches us to value relationships over accomplishments. Linking our value as families, employees, and church members to how busy we are seems to be the opposite of His plan for us.

Where do these "busyness equals godliness" ideas come from? Many years ago, in *The Protestant Ethic and the Spirit of Capitalism*, Max Weber wrote that the first capitalist economic systems and the Industrial Revolution in western Europe were partially shaped by the Protestant religious beliefs of the citizens—especially early Calvinism and Puritanism. John Calvin maintained that God selected some people for salvation and others for damnation. Early Calvinists regarded an individual's financial success as a sign of God's blessing. Those who were poor were seen as spiritually lacking. Calvinists were perhaps the first "workaholics" who strove to amass great wealth, for this was surely an outward sign of God's favor. When they became wealthy, instead of sharing their wealth with the poor, who were obviously doomed anyway, they reinvested their money for even greater wealth and "spiritual blessing."

Many of today's workaholics and hyper-scheduled families continue to link their value with their busyness. There's no time for family dinners or relaxing Sunday afternoons, because there's too much to do.

Weber maintained that a "Protestant work ethic" resulted, almost a kind of religion that linked success with God's favor. Early Calvinists were perhaps among the first to "hyper-schedule" themselves and to link busyness with goodness.[6]

Unfortunately, many of today's workaholics and hyper-scheduled families continue to link their value with their busyness. There's no time for family dinners or relaxing Sunday afternoons, because there's too much to do. Perhaps we will one day look back and wish we had slowed down long enough to "smell the roses"—or perhaps plant them. Some people already are.

In *Who Switched the Price Tags?* Tony Campolo tells the story of a group of elderly people who were asked what they would do differently if they could live their lives over. One of the top responses was "I would reflect more." One man even said he would take more baths and fewer showers. They implied they would slow down and enjoy life instead of speeding and "busifying."[7]

One way to do this is to trim down the schedule, omitting activities that are not absolutely necessary, and even those someone *thought* were necessary.

Katrina Kenison in *Mitten Strings for God* tells how her family began to simplify their lives. They began turning down invitations, turning off the noise (televisions, radios, stereos), and leaving time to do nothing together. They began to make "small shifts in thinking and behavior rather than full-scale self improvement."

One of these small shifts she and her husband made was to have their sons wait until they reached age 10 before they could join an organized baseball team. The boys and their father made up their own teams and played in their backyard instead. She admits that it takes tremendous self-control to create a home where quiet is valued and family time receives priority, but in the end the effort is worthwhile. Kenison states "at some point, we may begin to ask ourselves: Just whose standards am I living by, anyway? An advertiser's? A neighbor's? A parent's? A corporation's? When we stop long enough to figure out what we really care about and begin to make our choices accordingly, we can create lives that are authentic expressions of our inner selves. . . . When we race through life, we miss it."[8]

And so this is our challenge. How can we live in our 21st-century world and not be "of the world?" How can we avoid being caught up in a modern materialistic culture that tells us more is better? Is it possible to slow down, sit on the front porch, and get connected with our families, neighborhoods, and churches?

Yes, but it may not be easy. If we want to live in genuine community, we have work to do.

For Reflection and Discussion

1. Were you hyper-scheduled in elementary school, or did your parents limit your activities?

2. There are certainly positive reasons for encouraging children to be involved in activities, but what do you think could be the result of too much involvement for young children? What is the definition of too much?

3. Do you believe, as do some family counselors, that we're

teaching our children that something is wrong with relaxing? Do you think "busyness" has become a national status symbol? If so, provide examples.

4. Can you see how some people would see severely limiting children's activities as severely limiting their potential? Discuss.

5. Is something "magical" about eating together as a family? Did your family (or a family you know of) have regularly scheduled meal times, or did (do) you eat individually and on-the-go most of the time? Discuss the pros and cons of each.

6. The author speculates about what God must think about the busyness of our lives, and the guilt we feel if we miss an occasional church service because we're exhausted. If you've been raised in a conservative tradition, this may sound like heresy. What's your reaction?

7. It's been said that 20 percent of the members do 80 percent of the work in the church. Who loses in an arrangement like this? What can or should be done, if anything?

8. How have you (or could you) simplify your life? Do you see a need for this?

9. Why do you think we link our value as individuals (Christians) with our busyness? Do most of us think that if we don't do it, it won't get done?

10. Kenison maintains that "when we race through life, we miss it." What are some concrete ways we can slow down as individuals, families, neighborhoods, and communities of faith?

3

Cyberfreaks and Webmasters

The major advances in civilization are processes
that all but wreck the societies in which they occur.
—Alfred North Whitehead

"I know the plans I have for you," declares the LORD, *"plans to prosper*
you and not to harm you, plans to give you hope and a future.
—Jer. 29:11

All of us know people who seem to have been attached to a Pentium processor the day they learned to read. We come into contact with them occasionally, but they scare us. We feel lost the moment they open their mouths. They appear to be in a world of their own, and they seem to like it that way.

For whatever reason, some of these computer wizards choose to isolate themselves from friends and family and devote their time to their computers instead. Nearly every waking hour revolves around interaction with a machine. Their family relationships suffer, their spiritual lives are affected, and their work declines as they become shut off from actual face-to-face contact. Everybody has heard of, or even knows, someone whose marriage has ended because one of the partners could no longer be a partner: his or her time was completely devoted to meeting people via the Internet.

Today's computers are so user-friendly that they actually can be more appealing than the often-hostile world of human interaction. Most relationships and families, no matter how well adjusted, simply cannot compete with the lure of the World Wide Web. Researchers or alarmists, depending on where you stand, warn of carpal tunnel syndrome, eyestrain, isolation, depression, "e-strangement," and withdrawal from "real" people. A name even exists for this new "illness": Internet addiction disorder.

Yahoo magazine, defending the technological advances, reminds us that all modern conveniences were met with skepticism when they were introduced. In 1837, when the telegraph was first in use, warnings of "telegrapher's paralysis" were publicized. Typed letters were called "alienating and souless" by 19th-century critics. Believing the only way to communicate was in longhand, Anatole Broyard in the *New York Times Book Review* asked, "What can you express, after all, on a typewriter?" And television was criticized as an electronic babysitter, which we all worried would "soften our brains and make us socially inept." In 1978, *Newsweek* condemned the videocassette recorder (VCR) as a machine that would surely tear apart the American family.[1]

**Let's face it—it's too easy to become trapped
in the world of the computer and all the attachments
that have made our lives faster.**

Since most social changes are met with skepticism and, at times, alarm, we don't want to get carried away with irrational fears about the computer age. But we may have reason for concern.

Let's face it—it's too easy to become trapped in the world of the computer and all the attachments that have made our lives faster. Many of us can now be reached by telephone, fax, pager, answering machine, E-mail, mobile telephone, voice mail, or cell telephone at any hour of the day or night. We can be "up close and personal" at a moment's notice. We can "reach out and touch someone" (or be touched) wherever we go around the globe and in any time zone. We used to have only the telephone to answer at the office; now we have to respond to telephone messages, E-mail messages, pages, voice mail, and cell telephone calls. We used to cheerfully encourage each other to "stay in touch." Now we have no choice. We're hardly ever away from some means of telecommunication.

When we meet someone new, instead of exchanging phone numbers, we now have a long list of ways to reach each other. Business cards are even bigger to accommodate these expanded means of contact.

One creative innovation is the use of technology by church communities to help their members keep in touch during the week. A Houston church distributed beepers to congregants so they could send encouraging messages to a critically ill member. Since this person could not receive calls and personal visits, the members simply beeped their well wishes via a code system. Whenever the ill person's beeper sounded or vibrated with the code, he knew his church friends were praying for him.

Many nurseries in large churches now distribute beepers to parents so that in case of emergency the parents can be called to pick up their babies. This provides comfort to parents who are perhaps leaving their child for the first time, and it assures nursery workers that they will be rescued if the child becomes ill or is terrorizing the staff.

Another innovation involves the nursery staff assigning a number to each child. If a problem occurs during the service, the child's number appears on a screen in the sanctuary to notify the parents to pick up their child. One Sunday morning at our church we were convinced that an all-out mutiny was going on in the nursery when numbers appeared on the screen one right after the other and worried parents rushed out in mass exodus.

Those of us who don't actually want to be that accessible are looked at as rather strange. We're told that we're Neanderthals or old-fashioned, stuck in our ways, and that the world is passing us by. We're compared to the 19th-century Luddites, the British factory workers who resisted the introduction of technology to the textile industry. Afraid that the new, faster machines would cost them their jobs, the workers rioted, attacking their supervisors and destroying the machines. They had hoped they could hold onto a way of life that was simple, uncomplicated, and less mechanized. Of course, their resistance was futile, and after too many riots and too much bloodshed, several of the leaders were hanged and others were deported to Australia. (Let this be a warning to you!)

The word "Luddite," however, became synonymous with anyone who holds to the past and resists modern ways. So at the risk of being called a Luddite, some of us question whether we really do need all these means of communication. Yes, in an emergency these are nice options to have, but do we really need to be constantly connected? Does a burden come with this "cyber-umbilicus"? Or do the positives outweigh the negatives?

Only within the last decade have we come to "need" this much immediate contact with each other. Now, it seems, we can't live without it.

Today our computers allow us to file, edit, retrieve, view, insert, copy, print, scan, format, network, and use tools, tables, windows, and get 24-hour tech help from a real person. We can cut and paste, choose to save a document, or send a document to the virtual library, to our virtual briefcase, or the virtual trash bin. We can conduct most of our business via the computer terminal.

It may soon be possible never to have to stand in another line or interact with another civil service employee again. No more motor vehicle registration lines. No more standing in the wrong line at city hall for three hours. No more pushing our luggage in long lines at airports. Of course, it may be necessary to have our thumbprints scanned each time we cash a check at the local bank, even if we've known the cashier all our lives.

It's hard to comprehend that these advances in personal technology are actually relatively recent. Only within the last decade have we come to "need" this much immediate contact with each other. Now, it seems, we can't live without it. What did we ever do without E-mail? Without answering machines? Without call waiting? Without cell-phones? We all love to hear that chime and the friendly voice telling us "You've got mail"—until we find 265 messages waiting, most unsolicited and unwelcome "spam."

Cell phone users are everywhere today—in the theater, in church, in school classrooms, in business meetings, in check-out lines, and perhaps most precariously, behind the wheel of a car. It also appears that few cell phone users have taken Miss Manners' etiquette class, and few seem to be using their phones for emergencies, as cell phones are often marketed. Most are just chatting, making a list, or screaming at one child to stop hitting the other. Private phone conversation seems to have disappeared. Sharing personal information with everyone within hearing range has become commonplace.

The rest of us are treated to these private conversations whether we want to be or not. I love to be behind these people at the grocery store, for it makes my life appear so calm by comparison. I have yet to become important enough to need to be in constant contact with anyone else. My life is still so simple that conversations can wait until I get home with the bread and milk—although some days I can't remember that last item we need, and I admit, a cell phone might be nice.

Our desire to be connected has also introduced a whole new interactive language that is in constant flux as we race to keep up with the latest jargon. It takes the form of www, dot.com, nets, URL, org, edu, microchips, files, drives, conferences, group messages, corridors, cafés, live chats, networks, and the all-inclusive cyberspace. We have the Web, web pages, webcams, web design, webworks, web hosting, web development, web sites, and webmasters.

Then, of course, we now preface many of our new words with "virtual," meaning "the same for all practical purposes," creating phrases like "virtual reality," a classic oxymoron. We have virtual files, virtual television, virtual communities, virtual families, virtual relationships, virtual shopping carts, and virtual worlds. We can cybershop, have a cyber-relationship, conduct a cyber-interview, engage in cybersex, or visit a chat room. We have digital highways, digital computers, digital cameras, digital divides, digital families, and digital transfers. We can log on, interact, interface, access, prompt, uplink, search, download, scan, teleconference, videoconference, hack, crash, corrupt, freeze, reboot, and shut down. We have databases, CD-ROMS, DVDs, PCs, Apples, laptops, Palm Pilots, Playstations, laser disk players, search engines, floppy disks, hard drives, software, Pentium processors, broadbands, corrupted book sectors, and Powerpoint presentations. Our lives are affected by e-commerce, instant messaging, Internet access, Internet indexes, on-line shopping, computer consulting, viruses, and anti-viruses.

The "mouse" and "cat" are not what they used to be. Most of us use our computer mouse daily, and many of us are using the cue-cat to connect us directly to our chosen web sites without having to type the cumbersome web addresses.

Then there are the partisanships—Microsoft versus Macintosh versus Unix versus Linux, and AOL versus ATT Work-net versus Flash.net versus Compuserve versus MSN. There's Yahoo versus Google versus Lycos versus Hotbot and Netscape versus Internet Explorer. There's Ebscohost versus Infotrac versus OCLC-Worldcat.

In some circles, a person's status is linked to his or her knowledge, ability, and ownership of the latest personal technology with the right labels, greatest storage capacity, most power, and highest speed.

We all make statements about ourselves with the items we purchase, choose to drive, or wear. The area of personal technology is really no different. However, many social scientists warn of a "digital divide" separating the haves from the have-nots—those who can access and own the new technology and those who cannot.

Fortunately, many organizations now provide equipment and free Internet access to the poor and the homeless to bridge this divide. I was surprised during a trip to a remote area of Romania to find a free "Internet café" provided by a Christian university for its staff and students, also available to the many poor people in the town. Street people can come in for hot coffee and be introduced to the miracles of the Internet.

Ask any middle school student in the United States, and you'll find that he or she already has a favorite fast food, computer game, clothing brand, and athletic shoe.

As with all innovations, advertisers seek to connect with potential customers in order to make their products seem indispensable. One of the best techniques they use is to target the youth market, rationalizing that if young people get hooked on a product, they'll become lifelong consumers. As with soft drinks, chips, and pizza, technology manufacturers hope to establish strong product loyalty. Ask any middle school student in the United States, and you'll find that he or she already has a favorite fast food, computer game, clothing brand, and athletic shoe.

This marketing strategy works. The personal technology industry has used it to seek out even kids who are still in diapers. In a recent newspaper review called "My First Keystrokes," a writer recommended a program called "Jump Start Toddlers," by Knowledge Adventure. For just $29.99, parents can purchase software that "gets little ones as young as 18 months off to a solid start with catchy activities for learning letters, numbers, shapes, colors, and vocabulary."[2]

Whatever happened to carefree days of taking naps, sucking thumbs, and playing with blocks? We can also find numerous "How to Be Safe in Cyberspace" publications and workshops, many designed for children and sponsored by technology manufacturers. The children can learn how to be cautious on the Internet at an interactive computer play area set up at their local shopping malls.

Some of the most popular Internet sites promise a sense of community, a "place" you can find people just like you—a chat room or other interactive site that lets you communicate with others who have logged on and are ready to "talk." Most sites revolve around a specific topic or clientele, but not always.

In these places, "everybody knows your name," or at least the name you use that day. You can feel a part of the group for as long as you wish. You can pretend to be anything you want and describe yourself however you want. You can say anything, and if you're careful, no one will ever know who you are. It's the ultimate fantasy. You can even find how-to web sites that show you how to set up a community of your own, plus guidebooks for creating your own cyber-community.

Another development is the use of cameras that can give you immediate actual shots of a selected site. You can see a news event happening half a world away, or you can watch your two-year-old in his or her daycare center or your pet at the vet's office. These cameras, routinely used in the news media, are now being used by police departments to monitor city buses, trains, and street corners. And now you can pay a webcam fee, subscribe to the service, and view selected sites from your own computer.

On December 31, 1999, cameras were positioned in cities around the world as we ushered in a new year and the turnover of the calendar to 2000. People around the globe could view the celebrations live via satellite or webcast. For a few moments we truly seemed to be a global village, all celebrating together.

Most of us have these services available if we're willing or able to pay for them. But the best customers are those sometimes called "cyberfreaks," who will sit in a comfortable chair in front of a computer monitor for hours at a time. These are the people who buy all the latest computer products and keep up with the latest jargon. Their conversations are peppered with words that weren't even words a few years ago, using a language that's foreign to anyone unable to keep up.

They've learned that they can do just about anything online. They can find a job, find a house, find a mate, watch a movie, play chess, book a flight, hire an escort, take a college class, order junk food, order drugs, take a test, read the newspaper, or "experience" the news live. The virtual sites they visit are devoted to such topics as coffee, parenting, politics, horticulture, history, music, health care, and travel.

Most of these sites regularly solicit opinions and feedback. Participants feel they are important and are taken seriously. They also know they can have on-line discussions with someone in the next office or on the other side of the planet. The people participating in the virtual conversations may not even be who they say they are.

Of course, some people have always preferred to be alone, away from the crowd. Some would have been called "loners" long before the recent advances in personal technology.

What's new is the high rate of involvement in the pseudo-relationships available via the computer and the intensity with which these relationships are often pursued. What's also new is that more people seem willing to jeopardize their lives for relationships via the computer terminal. Some even give up their real marriages for long-distance "love" via the Internet. It's probably too early to declare this an epidemic, but it has been and will be a compelling phenomenon to watch.

This is probably a good time to point out that marriages have ended at about the same rate throughout much of the last 100 years or so. Despite today's chilling 50-percent divorce statistic that's the mainstay of news features and magazine articles, the rate of marriage dissolution has not actually changed much over the last century. What has changed is the most frequently cited reason *why* marriage ends. Today most marriages dissolve as a result of divorce, whereas in the past marriages more commonly ended as a result of one partner dying or as a result of one partner abandoning the other.

We should also remember that if about 50 percent of marriages end in divorce, about 50 percent do not—and that may be the more amazing statistic. With the many challenges confronting marriages, it may actually be more astounding that many couples stay together for the long haul. Today it's possible for a marriage to last 70 years or more. This was unheard of in the past, because most people simply didn't live that long.

Certainly, with longer life spans, the definitions of commitment and marriage are changing. What used to be a promise to spend 15 years together can now be a 50-year contract. It's probably not surprising that many people find this impossible to accomplish. And it probably isn't surprising that people in their 50s and 60s are choosing to divorce, for they realize that they could, with good health, spend another 25 years in an unhappy relationship.

What's new is that increasingly the computer plays a part in the failure of some marriages. When one partner withdraws from his or her spouse and family and finds more fulfillment with virtual relationships, it can easily result in trouble.

The Stanford Institute for Quantitative Study of Society found that one in seven on-line users is in danger of losing contact with "real human beings."[3] Researchers at Carnegie Mellon examined Net users in Pittsburgh over two years and found that frequent users were more likely to become depressed.[4] Psychologists at the University of Pittsburgh, comparing frequent Internet use with a gambling addiction, were the first to use the term "Internet addiction disorder" after a study of 396 regular Internet users and a control group of 100.[5]

Some of the these preliminary studies have been criticized for their design and methodology[6] and are likely less than perfect, but as we watch the expansion of the computer age into our personal lives, and as people become more technologically dependent, it will be interesting to examine the impact from these rapid social changes.

For Reflection and Discussion

1. Discuss examples of "e-strangement" and withdrawal from "real" people that you have observed.

2. What are some of the dangers of spending too much time surfing the net, and how can these dangers be prevented?

3. The author discusses other inventions (telegraph, typewriters, television) that received criticism when they were first introduced. What are some other examples?

4. The creative innovations that modern technology has introduced seem to outweigh its dangers and, as with any new idea, there are problems to be worked out. Do you agree? Are there other ways to measure technology's effects?

5. The Luddites and other groups warned of cultural changes

that would result when the changes in technology "trickled down" to how we live our everyday lives. Most of us don't want to go back to the days before the Internet, so how can we make our postmodern lives more community-like?

6. Do you foresee more laws, as some communities are already doing, to severely restrict the public use of cell phones? Should the rights of cell phone users prevail over those of non-cell phone users?

7. Discuss the dangers of the "digital divide." What might happen if the poor are left behind in the technological revolution?

8. The Internet has been blamed for the break up of many modern marriages, yet marriages in the United States are ending at about the same rate as a century ago (when abandonment and death figured more highly in the totals than today). What do you know about marriage breakups before 1950? Why do we believe marriage breakups are a new idea?

9. Marriages ending in divorce have increased in recent years. What do you know about the causes of divorce? What else do you think contributes to the rate of marriage failure in the United States?

10. Many cyberfreaks and webmasters scoff at the idea of "Internet addiction disorder." What do you think? Are some people actually "addicted?"

PART 2

Communities That Include Us

*If we want to rebuild community, then we must
seek communities that include us.*

Communities are made of members who share common
characteristics. The membership requirements could be
as simple as living within a particular subdivision and being
a member of a neighborhood association. It could involve
being a mother or father of a preschooler and belonging to
an organized play group. Or it could be religious beliefs that
make one denomination or congregation preferable to another.

We tend to belong to groups that have members who are
like us—they live where we do (our neighborhood), they
play the roles we do (parents), or they believe as we do (our
local congregation).

But if communities are made up of members who share
common characteristics, then nonmembers must also exist.
Most of these nonmembers have communities of their own,
communities with whom they share common characteristics.

But what about those who want to be a part of the faith
community? Do they feel welcome?

Perhaps they have much in common with the community but for some reason are not embraced by the membership.
Are there those who would be considered "the least of these"
and have traditionally not been welcome? And what's the responsibility of the community to embrace new members?

In Part 2, we focus on four groups (children, young
adults, the marginalized, and those in crisis) who may not feel

embraced by the community of faith and whom we need to make a special effort to include. If we are to build genuine "front-porch communities" we'll need to get to know our neighbors and learn how to include them in community life. If a society can be judged by how it takes care of its weakest members, the New Testament challenge to "love your neighbor" and to build communities that include them takes on new meaning in our rapidly changing world.

4

The Least of These

*It may not be possible for us to create a world
in which no innocent children suffer, but
it is possible to create a world in which
fewer innocent children suffer, and if we look
to the believers and don't find help,
where else will we go?*
—Albert Camus

*Whoever welcomes a little child
like this in my name welcomes me.*
—Matt. 18:5

When we think about our responsibility for children, it's easy to limit ourselves to the ones who live in our houses, live on our streets, or go to our churches. But perhaps we should expand our thinking to include a wider community and greater responsibility for the children around us.

Can we, as Christian communities, impact the lives of the children around us—even those we don't know?

Last year in my state 47 children died from abuse or neglect. Forty-seven children's lives were ended too early. Forty-seven children are gone. We shake our heads and ask ourselves how this could happen one time, let alone 47 times.

Where were the parents, teachers, pastors, health care workers, Sunday School teachers, social workers, and counselors in these children's lives? Where were the adults when these children cried out in hunger or pain? Where were the people of faith? What were we doing at the moment they died? And really, what does this have to do with us?

Our first inclination is to lash out at the parents and place the blame squarely on their shoulders. We demand that they be punished for hurting their children, for punching, slapping, shaking, burning, and kicking them so badly that the children are now dead. We condemn the parents for their unwillingness or inability to provide for their children, for leaving them at home alone, for not sending them to school, for failing to provide adequate food, clothing, and shelter, for failing to be good parents.

We buy our kids the best athletic shoes with the most popular logos, often costing as much as what some families in third-world countries live on all month.

Most children in North America are thriving, living healthy and happy lives while racing from soccer games to birthday parties to band practice. We buy our kids the best athletic shoes with the most popular logos, often costing as much as what some families in third-world countries live on all month. After all, it's worth it to spend $120 for shoes when we see our 10-year-old's beaming face. We feel proud.

Most of our children take vitamins and get nutritious meals. They have clean drinking water and bathe daily (whether they want to or not). When they're ill, we seek medical care. Our kids have the books and school supplies they need and even designer clothes with popular brand names.

Parents go to great lengths to entertain their children with video games, toys, movies, and trips. We pay for them to join organized sports leagues and send them to scout meetings and summer camps. Their rooms are so filled with gadgetry that being sent to your room certainly isn't what it used to be! On their 16th birthdays some get keys to new red sports cars. We tell ourselves, "All the other kids have them, and we don't want our kids to feel left out."

Most of our children have what they need and then some. And isn't that where our responsibility as parents should end? We gave birth to our national-average 2.5 children, and it's our job to care for them. We do the best we know how, even though we don't always know if what we're doing is the right thing. Like all good parents, we spoil our kids now and then and delight in watching them grow up. There's no greater joy than watching our children mature into the adults they are to become. But surely we're not responsible for others' children, especially those who aren't trying as hard as we are, those who don't seem to be taking the job as seriously as we are.

In our world you take care of yourself and your own, and you stay out of other people's business.

What can we do about what's happening in the house down the street? What business is it of ours anyway? Of course, we don't want anybody to get hurt, but we don't want to poke our noses into somebody else's affairs either. Something doesn't seem quite right with that family, but if that's how they want to run their household, it's no concern to us. Besides, this is a good area, and things like that don't happen here. If a problem existed, surely the authorities would be looking into it. We do say a prayer for that family when we pass by.

By now we've all heard the African proverb "It takes a village to raise a child," but something doesn't sound right about that for our modern culture. In our world you take care of yourself and your own, and you stay out of other people's business.

That's not how it used to be in those so-called "good old days." You've heard your grandparents tell you that if a child was rude to an adult, threw a rock through a window, or hit her little brother, any adult in the neighborhood had the right to discipline that child. In some neighborhoods, this even meant spanking. All the children in the neighborhood knew this and knew what to expect—and the parents did too. The parents agreed that their child must have deserved what he or she got if the neighbor saw what happened and punished all the kids.

Now we can imagine how much of our grandparents' accounts was fact and how much was embellishment, but these unwritten rules did exist in some areas, and they still do in some places.

For most of us, though, it's hard to imagine anybody punishing our child—even a member of our extended family. It's hard to let anyone tell us how to raise our kids. We won't stand for it. And perhaps this is what makes us hesitate to "interfere" with what occurs in our neighbors' home. We wouldn't want them to interfere in ours.

One prominent feature of North American society is the emphasis on individualism. A person's rights are protected by law and are sacrosanct. In response to totalitarian governments in other parts of the world, ours was established with built-in respect and protection for the individual. The small group of people who founded our country were adamant that individual freedoms should be protected, sometimes even at the expense of the majority.

Ironically, many of those who established the government of the United States and wrote the original documents about individual freedom owned slaves. Their proclamation that "all men are created equal" was not intended for Blacks (who were considered only $\frac{3}{5}$ of a person) or for women, who had few of the rights of citizenship.

In spite of this, our country's emphasis on individual freedom is one thing that draws people here. It's a characteristic we all appreciate about where we live. Individual freedom is part of the foundation of a democratic government and capitalist economy, but it impacts our personal lives in curious ways. It is at once one of the best characteristics of our society and one of the worst.

Only rarely do we get involved in our neighbors' private lives—and we do it then only with trepidation.

While other modern cultures place a greater emphasis on the good of the whole—the welfare of the entire family group, village, city, or society—ours places a greater emphasis on the good of the individual. We're encouraged to take responsibility for ourselves, to improve our own lives, and to be successful. When we're successful financially, we own that success. If in the process our success helps others, that's "icing on the cake." Competition is encouraged. As adults, it's every man and woman for himself or herself. That's one reason our economy has thrived.

It's also one reason we have some of our social problems. Everyone is responsible for his or her own home and family. Only rarely do we get involved in our neighbors' private lives—and we do it then only with trepidation.

This freedom allows for incredible personal choice and individual autonomy, but it also often results in isolation from those around us and in alienation from community. It makes us hesitate to become involved in others' lives. After all, we don't want anyone telling us how to live our lives, do we?

People in some parts of the world have a different mindset. The well-being of individuals and families is considered a national concern, a governmental responsibility. These societies allow extensive personal freedom, but if an individual or family is in trouble, it's considered the government's role to step in and repair the situation. In these social democratic societies, the good of the whole is emphasized instead of the good of the individual; the success of society is given preeminence over the success of the individual.

It might surprise you to learn that some of these societies are better off in terms of overall health and well-being than we are. The people of the United States, the strongest and most progressive nation in the world, like to think their country is far ahead of others in most areas, but when it comes to caring for children, Americans' overall track record is not so good.

In United States Census Bureau studies, the overall welfare of children and youth in the United States is compared with that of other modern countries around the world. It's surprising, but when these countries are ranked, the United States comes in near the bottom of the list. Of the countries compared in the studies, our record on overall child welfare is often among the worst.

Here's why the United States does so poorly. The research found that children in the United States are more likely to die in infancy, live in poverty, and be killed before they reach adulthood (age 25) than the children in many of the other countries.[1]

Let's be realistic. Perhaps we can't save the world, but surely we can do a better job than we've done in the past.

Some studies show that our infant mortality rate is twice as high as Japan's. We have the highest teen pregnancy rate, and we lead the more-developed nations in number of divorces. And when families need help financially, they're more likely to get adequate assistance in the other societies than in the United States.

A common reaction to this research is to challenge the data. It's not easy news to accept. Instead of imagining a world in which all of the nation's children could be doing as well as yours and mine, we mourn the truth that many of our children are doing poorly. It's hard for us even to imagine a different way of doing things.

What's the responsibility of the community of faith to address these issues? Can we effect change so that

—every expectant mother receives prenatal care?

—top-quality education for all in a safe environment is a reality?

—no one would have to live in substandard housing and drink contaminated water?

—taxes are used to build schools, libraries, and museums instead of prisons?

Let's be realistic. Perhaps we can't save the world, but surely we can do a better job than we've done in the past. Jesus told us to be concerned about the widows, the poor, the children, those in prison. He spent a lot of time talking about this, so we Christians have no choice but to be concerned about them in our neighborhoods, at our churches, and in the voting booth.

Some political leaders are echoing this concern. United States Secretary of State General Colin Powell maintains that "When parents need help or are absent, it's up to the rest of us to step in." He concludes, "We're too rich a nation to say we can't afford to provide health care to every child."[2]

Each of us benefits from taking care of the children around us. Their success helps us all in the end.

Here's the hard part for our families, neighborhoods, and churches—it may take us out of our comfort zones. We may have to be open to people who aren't like us. They don't look like us, they don't act like us, and they don't share our beliefs. It won't be easy to make a place for these weakest members of our community—the least of these. It may mean that the front porch gets a little crowded and a little noisy, but we may all benefit from the experience in the end.

For Reflection and Discussion

1. Should we as a community really have to take some of the blame for abused children? Isn't this a little extreme?

2. In the United States we tend to place the blame for child abuse and neglect on the shoulders of the parents or caregivers. How do other cultures share in the blame, and why? Provide examples.

3. While most children in the United States are thriving, about 25 percent are not doing so well. What do you think are the most serious "children's issues" in our society?"

4. We hear many people (government leaders, political candidates, social critics, theologians) tell us that "our children are our future," yet 25 percent live without what most of us consider the basics. To what extent is the government responsible? To what extent is the community of faith responsible?

5. The author says individual freedom is "one of the best characteristics of our society and one of the worst." Explain how this can be. What are the results? Does this emphasis on individualism actually cause social problems?

6. A disturbing report places the United States last in overall welfare of children and youth as compared to other modern countries. How does this last-place rating affect the well-being of the rest of U.S. society?[3]

7. How can we better meet the needs of our country's children?

8. The United States has more of its citizens behind bars than any other developed country, and we're building more prisons at a rapid rate. Explain why this is the case, and discuss why other societies are not doing the same.

5

Single-Serving Relationships

*Compare what you want with what you have,
and you'll be unhappy; compare what you have
with what you deserve, and you'll feel better.*
—Evan Esar

*What will it profit a man if he gains
the whole world, and loses his own soul?*
—Mark 8:36, NKJV

If our goal is genuine community, we will need to build communities that include the new adults—the 20-somethings, the "quarter-lifers," the generation X-ers. As older members of many church congregations have realized, their values are not necessarily shared by the 20-somethings. Their life goals and worldviews are unique, and their definition of worship is different. This is more than a generation gap—this is a challenge to the church to be more than "their father's church," to be a church that meets the needs of the new adults.

Why is this, and why do our church communities have difficulty reaching this age group? Let's look at the 20-something culture.

What about their entertainment? What do they watch these days? Many are watching movies like *Fight Club*—a film most Christians consider inappropriate and even vulgar. Nevertheless, it seems to have struck a chord with young adults. In this particular movie, a 20-something professional man discusses the futility of his life, the despair of his hopeless condition and that of most other people he knows. He feels adrift with nothing to hold onto, certain that who he is and his contributions are of little value to those around him.

As he travels around the country, he forms "single-serving relationships," which last only a few hours before he moves on to the next. He meets people on the plane whom he knows he'll never see again after the flight. The airline serves him an individual meal on his own individual tray, and he says, "Everything is a copy of a copy of a copy. . . . We are only consumers . . . lose an hour, gain an hour; this is your life, and it's ending one minute at a time."

This movie received mixed reviews, but several million young people saw it and talked about it. For some, the movie resonated their feelings of isolation, despair, and lack of "connection" with others.

To try to explain this, we can look back more than 100 years ago to Emile Durkheim, the French sociologist. His classic study of suicide, still recognized by social scientists, concluded that suicide is based on humans' need to be "connected." Although suicides occur for many reasons, Durkheim found that those who commit suicide are likely to be the least in touch with those around them—likely to need others and be needed by others the least.

Expanding his study, Durkheim also found that members of certain religious groups were much *less* likely than others to commit suicide. He found that Catholic and Jewish communities encouraged community to a greater degree and gave group affiliation a higher priority than most Protestant groups.[1]

Durkheim's research may have a message for our faith communities today. Although we hear a lot about teen suicides, older, retired men who may no longer feel needed are the ones most likely to take their own lives. We're also finding that religious affiliation does not protect us from divorce, since the rate is similar for those who identify themselves as religious and those who do not.

Durkheim warned that as societies modernize, they have fewer rules and tend to expand personal freedoms. Although this sounds good, and we relish the ability to make our own personal choices, this modernization process has a downside. Because modern and postmodern societies are complex, with a variety of races, cultures, and faiths, they often provide little moral guidance for individuals.

The characters in *Fight Club* experienced this—what Durkheim and others have called "anomie," a lack of collective rules to guide them. They were away from family and close friends; they were making money, more than they could spend, but they had no moral compass to guide their decision making.

Today in the "Silicon Valley" (California) and the "Microsoft Mecca" (Seattle), thousands are experiencing anomie, though they may not know what to call it. They are young, newly rich, and without a secure moral footing. Some have become very rich very fast and are without guidelines for how to live. Though many enjoy their newfound wealth and fame, others are finding it difficult to come to terms with their rapid success.

Many are spending some of their money on counseling for "sudden wealth syndrome." Though the rest of us may find this "disease" amusing (and most of us would be willing to trade our problems for theirs), for those living through these sudden changes, it's no laughing matter. Many who suffer this malady are fresh out of college, far away from their extended families, and are millionaires. They can afford, and are willing to pay, several times the asking price for homes in these areas as the real estate market cashes in on the technology boom. According to the *San Jose Mercury News,* 800-square-foot homes sometimes sell for as much as $750,000 in San Jose because of their location in Silicon Valley. Potential buyers have even brought "bribes" such as home-baked cookies and even airline tickets to an open house to persuade the sellers to take their offer on the house.

Many of the new homes being built in these areas (and other parts of the country) are architectural and technological wonders, giving their occupants an independence that most of us cannot comprehend. The people who live in these houses never have to leave, for they have everything they need right at home. They have no need for a community church or synagogue; some worship in their own home chapels, and some worship through technology. With their own high-tech security systems, they have little need for the local police. With home delivery of gourmet foods, they have no need for the supermarket and may never venture into one. They can swim in their private pools, play tennis on their private courts, and watch films in their private screening rooms. They can work at home most days and avoid the long commute to the office. They can do their banking and investing and take care of all their correspondence in front of their computers. If they teach their children at home, an increasingly popular alternative, they may not even know or care what's happening in the public schools. They don't have to—these things don't affect them. They have no interest in the local school bond election—it doesn't affect their family.

And with a staff who is paid to meet their every need, they may seldom venture outside their secure compound. They are, for all practical purposes, able to shut out the rest of the world. They are self-sufficient and self-reliant. Unfortunately, many of them are feeling the negative effects of this self-enforced isolation. Instead of "Home Sweet Home," for them it has become "Bunker Sweet Bunker."

Counselors are finding that for many of the newly rich, their home fortresses are not enough. They want more out of life; they want something that will give their lives meaning. Many are saying, and this wouldn't surprise Durkheim, that they miss interpersonal relationships not only for what they can gain from them but also for what they could potentially give to them. Not only do they need others, but they also need to be needed by others.

These days not just the rich and powerful are isolating themselves. Most of the rest of us are living in ways that provide us with independence from those around us.

Now don't get me wrong—not all of the newly rich are unhappy and wallowing in misery. Some, in fact, are wallowing in their money and laughing at the rest of us. But enough people are showing up at their therapist's office (or having a video conference with their therapist from the comfort of their own homes) that scientists have given these symptoms a name, and professionals in the social and behavioral sciences are focusing on this recent development.

Also, city officials are challenged by these individual high-tech fortresses within their city limits. Though city leaders may never come into contact with the inhabitants of these little kingdoms, when they do meet, the interests of the nouveau riche may supersede those of the surrounding community. This happened when many parts of densely populated California experienced power shortages, in part due to the extensive computer technology use in this area.

These days not just the rich and powerful are isolating themselves. Most of the rest of us are living in ways that provide us with independence from those around us.

Our homes have changed drastically from those of only 25 years ago. They may not be the mansions of the Silicon Valley, but we have all devised ways to become independent from those around us and to make our homes our "castles."

Today kitchens in the United States are bigger and better equipped than ever before, and yet we cook in them less. Millions tune in to the Food Network's cooking programs, but the average adult in the United States eats out at least once each day, spending an average of $4.58 for each meal. We like to watch other people cook on television, but we just don't seem to want to go to all that effort ourselves. We don't even have to cook for the holidays. We can eat out or have complete holiday meals, the turkey and all the trimmings, delivered to the table in time for our guests to arrive.

Not only do we spend millions to buy houses, but in 1999 in the United States we spent $200 million to make dream homes out of them, places we would go to get away from it all, to relax and to be ourselves.

We are also going to great expense to protect ourselves and our possessions with elaborate security systems. The home security industry has made a killing on this need to protect our stuff.

We are tuning in to the cable network Home and Garden Television to find ways to enhance our "bunkers" ourselves. We furnish and equip them not only to be comfortable places in which to live, but as the hosts on these programs remind us, we need to keep in mind that "our homes reflect our personalities and are actually extensions of ourselves." They tell us that our homes reveal a lot about us, by the way we select furnishings and decorate our living spaces, so we spend millions "updating" our residences.

We also are taking on do-it-yourself projects that allow us to spend time and effort feathering our nests. Arthur Blank, the chief executive officer of Home Depot, has built 900 stores in three years in the United States, with 1000 more stores planned in the United States and Latin America. Nearly every large city in the United States now has one of the big orange "cathedrals" of home tools and supplies. At one time the company claimed that a new store was opening every 43 minutes. These "toy stores for dads" are now drawing women, too, and thousands attend the "Home Depot University" each year to learn how to enhance their homes themselves.

Though all of us desire a personal space that allows us to escape the demands of our public lives and a place we can call our own, perhaps we're going a little too far in seeking independence.

Not everyone is pleased, however; small, local hardware stores around the country complain that they simply can't compete with such megastores. In Wheaton, Illinois, community members protested the building of a Home Depot with a petition drive, and the chain dropped plans to build in that area.

Formica countertops are now a thing of the past as we demand marble or granite—materials our ancestors reserved for churches and cathedrals. Though all of us desire a personal space that allows us to escape the demands of our public lives and a place we can call our own, perhaps we're going a little too far in seeking independence.

It's probably not surprising that many people feel alienated in today's postmodern societies. Though some, like the newly rich, may choose to isolate themselves, and many of us isolate ourselves by creating a living environment that allows us to be independent, some are kept out of the mainstream for other reasons. Many feel marginalized, on the sidelines, left out because of their race, economic standing, or beliefs.

A good illustration for this is a sheet of notebook paper, the kind that usually has a red line running down the left side. Where does the action usually take place on that sheet of paper? Where are you most likely to write if you're taking notes in a class or making a list? Not in the margin! If you're typing a school paper or a letter on your computer, what happens in the margin? Not much!

People who feel marginalized, for whatever reason, feel left out. They aren't where things are happening. They're on the fringe. Another way of thinking about this is to envision a football game, in which the actual game takes place on the field, not on the sidelines. The people on the sidelines (coaches, trainers, cheering squads, bands, and fans) are important, but what the fans pay to see is what's happening on the field, not on the margins.

The popular and well-respected pastor . . . once told me he had been invited into only two of his parishioners' homes— after serving as their pastor for more than eight years.

A friend of mine who just started attending a new church commented on how it was different from those he had previously attended. Discussing what he observed as a lack of community feeling, he called this church a "collection of autonomous individuals." This didn't surprise me, for I've heard it many times. The people who attend this church may come to one, two, or three services each week, but many never connect with others who are sitting in the same pews. Some people center their family life around the church and could not relate to what others see as a lack of community feeling. But some are in the margins, sometimes even the leadership.

The popular and well-respected pastor of this church once told me he had been invited into only two of his parishioners' homes—after serving as their pastor for more than eight years. People invited him to eat at a restaurant and paid for his meal, but he was rarely invited to share a meal in their homes. This church of 1,000+ is financially sound, the sermons are scripturally based, and much good work is happening in and around the church—but there doesn't appear to be a sense of community, at least not for everyone.

It may surprise you that this is precisely why some people attend that church—for they are not looking for a church body to embrace them. They want to attend, but not to get involved, and they don't want follow-up calls and visits. Single-serving relationships are what they want, and that's what they often find in a church this size. It's safe to say not everyone is looking for a church that feels like a family or provides a close-knit community. The need for others' company and the need for community varies from individual to individual. What one individual or family needs from a church may be different than what others need. We're not all alike.

If we claim, however, that our communities of faith are more than "collections of autonomous individuals," and if we strive to provide more than "single-serving relationships" in our congregations, then we had better fulfill these promises. These are claims that are not taken lightly by those looking for a welcoming congregation, and this provides a challenge that nearly every church staff wrestles with at one time or another.

What sometimes makes the difference between "community" congregations and groups of "autonomous individuals" is the opportunities for involvement made available by the church leadership. The pastor and church leaders providing many and varied chances for service within the church can be a giant step toward creating a community atmosphere. When new members join my church, they are asked which ministry they want to participate in, and then, when they're introduced to the congregation, the pastor announces where this new person plans to get involved—the choir, children's church, youth work, program planning, and so on.

This doesn't work for everyone, but it sends a message to new members that they are welcomed and encouraged to become involved in a small-group ministry of the church.

Of course, I have a friend who attends my church who says he's happy for the numerous activities and programs of the church, but he's not interested in being involved in any of them himself. He'll support them with his offerings, and he'll pray for their success, but he just wants to attend the services and not be part of any small group. He's single but is not interested in any of our church's single activities. It's not "his thing." He also believes going to church too much can be harmful to your health. He says God didn't intend for us to go to church eight times a week.

For those who isolate themselves, and for those who are isolated by their circumstances, the Church has a mandate to be ready with doors and arms open when they do come calling.

For Reflection and Discussion

1. Even if you haven't seen the movie *Fight Club*, you may have heard of its graphic scenes of violence. Many social scientists warn that repeatedly watching violent acts on film (whether in news footage or movies) desensitizes us over time. Do you agree? Why or why not?

2. What do you think about the increase in the number of support groups in American society? What do you think is the cause of the growth in this industry?

3. In the article "Bowling Alone: America's Declining Social Capital" the author says our society increasingly encourages independent activities in all areas of our lives.[2] What are some ways our culture facilitates aloneness?

4. Durkheim maintained that a person's "chances" of committing suicide is impacted to some degree by his or her religious affiliation. Why do you think Catholics and Jews are less likely to commit suicide than Protestants?

5. Why are older, retired men most likely to take their lives? Besides individual effects, what does our culture tell them about

their usefulness? Why men and not women? Why whites and not people of color?

6. Most of us scoff at the idea of wealthy people suffering from "sudden wealth syndrome." But if a significant number are seeking therapy for this new malady, what does this say about our culture? What conclusions can we draw?

7. City leaders in Seattle find that many of the newly wealthy living in self-sufficient mansions no longer depend on the city's services, such as police, firefighters, utilities, and schools. What challenges does this cause for cities of the future?

8. Is anything wrong with eating out every day? Is anything wrong with spending money on our homes? Is anything wrong with paying others to do what our ancestors did for themselves?

9. Can you think of any examples of how we worship our homes? Are we really building cathedrals instead of castles? Explain the differences.

10. Is your church community a true fellowship, or is it more like a "collection of autonomous individuals?"

6

Not in Our Town

Witness always. Use words when you have to.
—Francis of Assisi

*What does the LORD require of you? To act justly
and to love mercy and to walk humbly with your God.*
—Mic. 6:8

It was just a tiny menorah in a window. A small Jewish boy
in Billings, Montana, had placed his menorah with the
candles lit in his window for the Hanukkah holiday. Few
Jews live in Billings, but the family thought nothing of dis-
playing this religious symbol. Before long, however, they received a message from one of their neighbors—in the form
of a brick through the window, destroying the menorah.

This criminal act was reported in the local newspaper,
and one Christian man decided to do something about it. In
the window of his business, he displayed a paper menorah he
had drawn himself. Before long, paper menorahs were in the
windows of Christians all over town. The people of Billings
were saying "Not in our town; we will not allow intolerance
like this in our community. We don't want to see others' beliefs trampled."

When I heard this story, I remembered "bricks" that have
been thrown in other communities. I thought of Ryan White
in Florida, whose home was burned to the ground because
of his HIV status; of Mathew Shepherd in Wyoming, who
was beaten, tied to a fence, and left to die in the cold night
because someone hated him because of his homosexuality; of

James Byrd in Texas, who was dragged to death by admitted racists because of his skin color.

Certainly not all of the citizens of Montana, Florida, Wyoming, or Texas are brick-throwers. Entire communities cannot be blamed for the actions of a few.

Are there times that our behavior, as individuals or groups, is too exclusive because those around us are just too different for us to accept?

And yet what about where we live? Surely this could never happen in our communities. We would never pick up a brick and hurl it through a window. We would never burn someone's house because he or she had a disease we didn't fully understand. Physically attacking someone, no matter how much we disliked or disagreed with him or her, is out of the question.

But perhaps we should ask ourselves, "Are there times that our behavior, as individuals or groups, is too exclusive because those around us are *just too different* for us to accept?" Their beliefs, behavior, dress, actions, or lifestyles are too "out there," and for some reason we think we must express our disapproval.

If we're really honest with ourselves, all of us hold "bricks" and may be ready to throw them if given the right opportunity. Some of us do this already and don't even know it.

What are some of these "bricks" we seem unwilling to give up? What opinions, beliefs, or prejudices do we hold that result in walls being built between our community and those on the outside? Why aren't we more willing to include those who are different from us? And what will it take to convince us to put down our bricks?

We must remember how important it is in our society (and in most societies) to fit in and to be included as a part of the group. Most of us don't realize the powerful peer pressure to conform that we all face—not just as adolescents, but throughout our lives.

One of the innovations in education in recent years has been an emphasis on experiential learning. Instead of sitting in the classroom, listening to lectures, and taking notes the entire semester, students are encouraged to _experience_ the topics they are learning about.

Sometimes this involves internship experiences through which students get a taste of the real world. But in my freshman sociology classes, experiential learning takes the form of the "breaking the norm" project. Instead of being "normal" and behaving like everyone else, students are told to do something that will set them apart or draw attention to them in some way. Then they are to report to the class what happened. Students have been creative with this project, and they come back to class with reports of bizarre incidents and startled reactions from bystanders.

One student decided to wear his clothes backwards. He said he was stopped repeatedly by strangers who asked, "Do you know your clothes are backwards?"

When you get on most any elevator in North America, you'll find that the passengers walk to the back, face forward, and stare up at the floor numbers.

Another entered an elevator facing the other riders and was overly friendly. She said people left the elevator as quickly as they could to get away from her. Another student went to an Italian restaurant and ate her spaghetti with her hands. One young man turned his chair around and faced the back of his college classroom instead of facing his professor. The professor was not pleased.

As you might imagine, this assignment is a popular one

that gets everybody laughing, and all the students are anxious to share their experiences when they return to class. They quickly realize, however, how much emphasis society places on conformity and how uncomfortable it is when they're different from everyone else. No etiquette rules are posted in elevators, and yet when you get on most any elevator in North America, you'll find that the passengers walk to the back, face forward, and stare up at the floor numbers. When you turn around in a crowded elevator, look at everyone, and start talking, you're definitely seen as abnormal. Try it yourself—you'll see. People will think you're nuts!

Amazing!

So it probably should not surprise us that once we become part of any group, distinctions are drawn between those who belong and those who don't. This is where the bricks come in. In order to build solidarity and group loyalty, comparisons will be made between those who are "in" and those who are not. Every group, large or small, has its own rules and regulations—whether we're talking about a family, a country club, a denomination, a local church, or a large corporation. In our family, when one of the kids questioned why our rules were different from those of the kids down the street, we often said, "You're a Wilcox. You're a part of the Wilcox family, and these are the Wilcox rules."

Unfortunately, though, it's sometimes just a short distance between making comparisons and assuming that members of our group are superior to those on the outside. And unfortunately, sometimes *comparisons* become *bricks*.

But how can we organize ourselves into faith communities? How can we have rules and regulations for membership in our group *and* be open to those on the outside? Is it possible to be both inclusive and exclusive? Do we want to?

This is an extremely difficult challenge. Many churches and faith-based groups have few rules for membership and will accept just about anyone who wants to become part of the group. Most of the church communities I've been in, however, have held fairly restrictive standards for inclusion in the group. You have to be willing to give up certain behaviors, take on certain new ones, and conform to the organization's rules.

Some conservative denominations in the North America regularly "duke it out" in the media as a result of their stands on particular issues. News reporters seem to wait with bated breath for these controversies, and critics pronounce these denominations as totally out of step with how most people in our culture live.

These media frenzies remind us of the media grandstanding in the 1970s and 1980s, when many conservative Christian families and congregations became involved in political issues for the first time. They gathered in informal living room sessions, group meetings, and at their churches to voice their disappointment with political leadership. Some of the informal groups became larger political organizations and eventually came to be called "the religious right."

In the last 20 years American politics have been significantly influenced by these groups of conservative Christians. The individuals, groups, and organizations that comprise this large conservative population have brought many social problems into public attention. Efforts by conservative Christian groups to influence legislation on abortion, school prayer, the Equal Rights Amendment, textbook censorship, pornography, and other issues are well documented. Christian individuals and groups have taken their place at the political table, and many of these groups remain active.

These groups have done much good in American society, and their positive influences on politics are without debate. What makes some Christians uncomfortable, however, is that these political groups are sometimes presented as "holier" than everybody else, as if they have the monopoly on what God says.

With apologies to Dale Carnegie, is this any way to "win friends and influence people"? My friends in the field of communication tell me that if you begin a new relationship with "I'm glad to meet you, but you're wrong" this could be interpreted as building a wall instead of a bridge. In *Bridges, Not Walls: A Book About Interpersonal Communication,* John Stewart says that interpersonal communication is contact between people. He adds that in order to establish contact, genuine interpersonal interaction with each other, we may need to accept those with whom we come in contact as they are and not how we would like them to be.[1] This is not easy, nor is it even always the only approach, but does it perhaps offer a lesson for those of us in conservative Christian denominations who too often appear to set ourselves above the rest of society? I know it's not as simple as that, but "I'm glad to meet you, but you're wrong" can't be the best approach. There must be a better way.

And maybe we can learn from our mistakes. Those of us who grew up in the United States during the 1950s and 1960s could not avoid the volatile issues of race, and I continue to be intrigued by these compelling topics of study.

For a period in the 1960s, our evening news was full of reports of Black and White confrontations and the violent struggles that came to be called the Civil Rights Movement.

These conflicts have been referred to as the "American dilemma," and many people have referred to the inequalities as our society's greatest shame. Whether we like it or not, these racial struggles are a part of our national legacy, and unfortunately it appears that we still have a long way to go toward racial reconciliation.

Each fall semester in a class called Race and Ethnicity, I introduce a group of predominantly white, middle-class, Christian students to these powerful and often shameful issues. In the first few weeks the class is collectively stunned. Most of the students were born long after the civil rights struggles of the 1960s, and they unfortunately know little about the events of that period.

Early in the class, after being immersed in the stories and pictures of what happened, many class members are reeling. Their reaction papers reflect this as they write, "I had no idea," "I've never heard of these events," "Why hasn't anybody ever told us about this?"

We don't want to know that fellow Americans have been despised, mistreated, and some even killed because of their skin color.

Most are intrigued by their research, and many tell me this is a favorite class, but they're also worried. Much of what they are learning goes against what they've been taught by their families and, tragically, by their churches. They're concerned about the discussions they plan to have when they go home for the holidays. I warn them that this topic can put a damper on conversation at the Thanksgiving holiday table (and they tell me it does). They relate conversations with racist relatives and friends and tell me about how this new knowledge has isolated them at times.

The best way I can explain this to them is to say that this information is "hard to hear." We don't want to know that fellow Americans have been despised, mistreated, and some even killed because of their skin color. Nearly every semester I have one or two students who *won't* hear it. It's frequently a well-to-do white person who comes to every class, sits down front, but consistently has a puzzled frown on his or her face. The questions are nearly always the same: "Why don't these people just accept things the way they are?" "Why do they [Blacks, Hispanics, Native Americans, Jews, women] have to make trouble?" Fortunately, I never have to answer these questions. Others in the class who would like to pummel their fellow student usually restrain themselves and kindly point out that maybe "walking a mile in someone else's shoes" might help us to understand where these groups are coming from. Students often do the best teaching.

Most figure it all out for themselves by the end of the semester, but some never do. Last year a student left our Christian university because his racist ideology and violent proposals for fixing America's problems, which he wrote about regularly in his freshman essays, were not being well received by his professors and the other students. He didn't think our university was the place for him. Though I had never met him, I was sorry to hear he was leaving, because he missed an opportunity to learn of God's all-encompassing love and care for His children of all races.

Our challenge is to find ways to teach our children to accept those who are different from us—those who look, act, behave, or believe differently.

Some people say the most segregated hour of the week is on Sunday morning, the hour that many of us are in church. Today some congregations still refuse membership or fellowship to people of other races. Surprisingly, some Christians don't see a problem with blending racism and Christianity, as if the two coexist. My students are shocked when they conduct an informal survey asking people in a community if it's possible to be a Christian *and* a racist, and many people respond yes. They are also surprised to learn that many men who once rode with the Ku Klux Klan on Saturday nights, terrorizing Black families in the South, actually attended church on Sunday mornings, some teaching Sunday School. They struggle with how these contrasting beliefs can be held by the same individuals, and they fear that they go to church now with some people like this.

In 1957 at Central High School in Little Rock, Arkansas, a white man picked up a brick and hit a Black news reporter

on the head with it. Like many Whites around the country at
that time, he was against integration, a policy that would allow Black students to attend school with white students. He
was on the street that day to express his outrage, and a news
camera recorded the event. The first time I saw that film
footage, I wondered, "What would it take to get me to pick
up a brick and hit another person? How angry or frightened
would I have to be? What would have to be at risk?"

All of us who want to build genuine, caring communities
of faith in our world can find a lesson in this. Our challenge
is to find ways to teach our children to accept those who are
different from us—those who look, act, behave, or believe
differently.

While it's important to hold fast to our standards, we
have to find creative ways to extend an open hand of fellowship to those outside our community, but we'll have to lay
down our bricks to do it.

For Reflection and Discussion

1. Discuss situations in which you would pick up a hypothet-
ical "brick." Would you ever actually be willing to pick up a brick
and throw it?

2. Where do you "draw the line" when accepting others, even
though you don't accept their behavior?

3. Consider "breaking a norm" to see just how much each of
us wants to be considered normal and be part of the group. What
happened? How did you feel?

4. What rules did your family (or a family you know) have
that were different from those of your friends and/or neighbors?
What was your reaction to these rules?

5. Is it possible for a faith community to be both inclusive _and_
exclusive? Can they hold their beliefs without being seen as "holier than thou"? Should they even be concerned about this?

6. Some people believe that religion and political activism don't mix, and others (often seated on the same church pew) believe they have to comingle. Where do you stand and why?

7. Besides the Civil Rights Movement, what other social movements can provide instruction for us as we seek to build community?

8. One of the most common suggestions for building genuine, caring communities is that we begin to teach our children to accept those who are different from us. Is this unrealistic? Are we expecting too much?

9. Should we be concerned that Sunday morning is one of the most segregated hours of the week? How have some Christian groups achieved racial reconciliation within their ranks and beyond?

7

A Death in the Family

Trust in him at all times, O people;
pour out your hearts to him, for God is our refuge.
—Psalm 62:8

Grieving is as natural as crying when you are hurt,
sleeping when you are tired, eating when you are hungry, or sneezing
when your nose itches. It is nature's way of healing a broken heart.
—Brennan Manning

It was 3 A.M. on a cold January morning five years ago, and I was in the intensive care unit of a small hospital near Lewisburg, West Virginia. The only sound I heard was two people snoring, very loudly and in unison. My father was in the hospital bed, and my mother was asleep on a cot, and they were snoring together. It's a good memory. My dad passed away three days later, and now, each time I think of my parents' hospital snoring competition, I smile.

My parents were married in 1946, when my dad returned home after serving in World War II, and they lived together for 50 years. Like most couples who married during this time, they immediately started a family and soon had four children. Neither of my parents graduated from high school, which was common during that time and in that part of the country. They were, however, determined to provide a good upbringing for their children, and they did well.

When the four of us children were quite small, we moved to a new house, and a neighbor dropped by to invite us to church. Over the years, the church became a second home to us; our lives revolved around its services and activities. If the doors were open, we were there. My parents taught classes and held leadership positions, and the church even let me sing in the choir—lack of talent notwithstanding. We attended Sunday School, Vacation Bible School, revivals, and church camps as if the success of these events depended on our being there.

If we're a genuine community of believers, at some point it becomes our responsibility to care for community members in pain.

When my dad died, the people of the church organized a massive community effort to support our family. The wake was held on a Sunday night, and the entire congregation was at the funeral home. They had to be—that's where the church bus took them.

They brought more food than we could have eaten in a month. They sent flowers—large arrangements and small hand-picked bunches. They surrounded us with their love and caring.

I had moved away from this church community many years earlier, and I had seen many instances of community-in-action, but none had been quite like the people in this little rural church in the West Virginia mountains. But in every community, crisis events occur. If we're a genuine community of believers, at some point it becomes our responsibility to care for community members in pain. One of the most challenging experiences to help someone through is the grieving process.

About 10 years ago, the university dean at my college asked me to develop a course called Death and Dying. My reaction was not entirely enthusiastic, since I knew nothing about the topic and wasn't especially interested in learning any more about it, even in the academic sense. Like many people my age,

I had not yet experienced the death of a close relative or friend, and I didn't want to jinx that by studying the topic. So you can imagine my surprise when I heard myself saying, "How interesting! Of course I'd be honored to accept this challenge." This is how university professors are trained to talk to their deans. Later that week I began the research.

The next year, I offered my first class called Death and Dying, and I'm still teaching it at both a Christian college and at a large state university. That first class had only 12 brave students; however, the next time we offered it there were 50, and we had to close the enrollment early because we ran out of chairs in the classroom.

I'm amazed that people sign up for this class, especially since we offer it each year in an intersession, the last two weeks of May. On the first day I always ask the students why they enrolled in the class. Usually I say, "Why in the world are you here? It's beautiful outside, you're young and healthy, and surely have better things to do. Why aren't you out enjoying life instead of sitting in here for two weeks talking about death?"

We've been labeled a "death-denying" society, because we avoid talking about death, as if this will keep it from happening to us or to anyone we care about.

The answers vary: some are planning on careers in medicine, others want to go into social work, and a few have had a recent death in the family—but most say they're _just interested_. They say it sounds intriguing, and they want to know more about it. They also say it's a topic no one has ever discussed with them, and feel a need to talk about it. I ask them about their families' and friends' reactions, and it's almost unanimous—the friends and families are concerned, as if studying the topic will bring bad luck.

At the end of the two-week session, the students always indicate that they have learned a great deal about how our society deals with death. Almost all have come to terms with how they view death, and most are more comfortable talking about it.

Surprisingly, this has become one of my favorite classes to teach, probably because I learn so much from my students each time. Those in the class come from a variety of cultures and religions, so we always have new perspectives and traditions to discuss—like that of the student from Brazil who believed that life is like a ride up an escalator, and when you die you simply drop off at the top; or the Hindu student who stressed how important it was to dress the deceased well for the entry into the next life so he or she could make a good impression. We also share many funeral stories—some hilarious, many tragic and heartbreaking.

Death is a topic we're only now learning to talk about in our culture. We've been labeled a "death-denying" society, because we avoid talking about death, as if this will keep it from happening to us or to anyone we care about.

We no longer nurse sick family members but turn them over to people who are professionally trained.

However, our society has not always been like this. Because most of our ancestors lived on farms, they experienced many deaths in the home with the family present. Burial took place on the family farm. For the most part, the realization was accepted as a matter of fact that not all the children in a family would make it through the first few years of life. Some social scientists have even theorized that before the 20th century, many parents hesitated to become too emotionally attached to their young children, knowing that some of them would probably die.

The births and deaths of farm animals were also a part of the routine of farm life, and the family saw this firsthand. By the time our grandparents reached adulthood, they had seen birth and death many times and probably were more straightforward in discussing it, even if they perhaps understood it less.

We may be more likely to understand the causes of death today, but we're much less accepting of it. Because of advances in medical science and technology, we believe we can stave off death, and we've done that as we've steadily increased the life expectancy of our population. We now live longer and healthier lives, and it's probably not surprising that we consider death a defeat. We don't want to admit that death's timing is outside our control. And tragically, we sometimes keep individuals alive long after they would have naturally died, often subjecting them to expensive, and perhaps needless, tests and procedures.[1]

We also tend to leave the "work" of death to professionals. We no longer nurse sick family members but turn them over to people who are professionally trained. Our insurance will pay, and we request that everything be done to save our loved one. This often results in more money being spent on health care for the average American during the last six months of life than all he or she spent during a whole lifespan.

When death happens, professionals direct the funeral and disposal of the remains. Seldom do family members play an active role in the process. It's not surprising, then, that we don't want to talk about death and dying or deal with it firsthand.[2]

At one time in our culture we didn't say the "s-word" (sex) or the "d-word" (death). Today we talk about sex much more often—many would say it gets entirely too much attention—but we still have difficulty talking about death. At the greeting card shop, even sympathy cards don't use the "d-word." They talk about a "loss." We can read poems and words of comfort, but even Hallmark rarely mentions that a death prompted the card in the first place.

If we're to be a genuine community of believers, we must learn how to get past our fears, confront our insecurities, and be available to others during this most dreaded experience. I've heard people say, "What would I have done without my church family when my husband died? What do people do who don't have this supportive network?"

A genuine "community of believers" comes to the aid of those experiencing their most desperate moments, even if they don't always know how to do it right. Grief counselors suggest that being present, even if we don't know what to do or say, is the best approach.[3] Simply being available to listen may be the greatest gift we can give when someone we know is grieving.

In my community, people turn out for funerals. We may not know how to talk about it, but we show up. This may be the best medicine for the family and for us.

Grieving typically lasts months and even years. The family and close friends will need long-term care and comfort.

Shortly after I moved here 20 years ago, the husband of an older faculty member died suddenly. That afternoon I received a call telling me to bring a salad to the faculty member's home as soon as possible. I mumbled that I would be happy to do that. My husband and I showed up at the house that afternoon, along with most of the community. The kitchen was full of women from the church, and some of the men were mowing the lawn. There were six other salads (all of which put mine to shame), and our grieving friend was already surrounded with a houseful of people who cared about her.

Unfortunately, much of the care we provide often takes

place in the week surrounding the death and funeral. We overwhelm the family for the first few days, and many of them are actually relieved when the funeral services are over, all the food is eaten, and everyone goes home. The grieving process continues, however, and the coming weeks and months may be the most difficult.

Most people think that the grieving process should last only a couple of weeks. After this, we expect the family to get on with their lives. Some of us even avoid talking with them, since they often only want to talk about the family member who has died.

However, grieving typically lasts months and even years. The family and close friends will need long–term care and comfort. This is where the genuine community of believers can focus their efforts, during the longer period of mourning.

At one time grieving relatives were required to dress in black for a specified length of time—often several months—to let everyone know they had experienced a loss. Anyone seeing them knew immediately that these individuals could not participate in social events, athletic activities, or parties because they were "in mourning." They were set apart from the rest of society and treated differently until a respectable length of time had passed—then they could shed their mourning clothes and "get on with their lives." We look back on this practice and consider it ridiculous and far too limiting, but we may actually be missing out on an important part of the grieving process. We may be asking others to get back to living too soon.

Perhaps it would be more healthful for all concerned if, when we were in mourning, we could be excused from most of our daily responsibilities for a required mourning period. During this time everyone would know that we were hurting and were to be handled with care. I'm not so sure I want to advocate "sackcloth and ashes" or even required mourning attire, but I do think we too often rush people through this process. One counselor told me many of the clients he sees are basically dealing with unresolved grief and loss—they have not been allowed, or have not allowed themselves, to adequately process their loss.

As a community of faith, we must develop strategies for dealing with crisis experiences like death when they occur within our fellowship. Each community of faith, whether large or small, must have a plan of action to meet the immediate and long-term needs of its members. In many churches, this involves the pastor or a staff member meeting with the family at the time of death and shortly thereafter.

What is too often missing, however, is the follow-up plan. We assume the individual's family and close friends will be there in the difficult times ahead—anniversaries, birthdays, and especially holidays. This may not be happening, and tragically, individuals and families have left the church because they did not receive the assistance they needed during these crisis times. A person faces no lonelier time than being in "the valley of the shadow of death."

One of the most common mistakes a congregation makes is to depend entirely on the pastoral staff to provide immediate and long-term services to those who are mourning.

The community of faith can in a variety of ways serve their members who have experienced a death. The best place to start is with training. A large congregation (or a combined effort of smaller churches) can provide grief counseling preparation for the pastoral staff and for volunteers interested in being in this ministry. These sessions, conducted by a psychologist, grief counselor, funeral service director, or a team of individuals, can be invaluable to the church community during the crisis and in the following months. These individuals, who regularly deal with terminal illness, death, and dying, are frequently called upon to counsel the bereaved and can provide practical suggestions for what to do when death occurs.

One of the most common mistakes a congregation makes is to depend entirely on the pastoral staff to provide immediate and long-term services to those who are mourning. Many assume that this is their job. Unfortunately, bereavement counseling may not "come naturally" to pastors—most of whom have had only limited seminary preparation for dealing with these events. In a large congregation, the pastoral staff may conduct several funerals each month and provide follow-up support for the families. These staff members would gladly welcome trained volunteers from their congregation to help provide these services.

Certainly, when a death occurs in the church family, it's a time for that community to move into action. It's been said that when a birth occurs we rejoice, when marriage takes place we celebrate, but when death occurs we do nothing. If there's one time when we should feel God's presence in the comfort of those around us, this is the time. This comfort could make all the difference to the Body of Believers—individually and collectively.

Last night I visited the Oklahoma City Bombing Memorial, commemorating the April 1995 terrorist event that tore apart the Murrah Federal Building in my city. Like everyone here, I remember where I was when the bomb exploded. It was a Wednesday at 9:01 A.M., and I was standing in my college classroom beginning a lecture to a group of freshmen. Little did we know what was to follow as the back wall of the room rumbled and shook a row of chairs—and we were 10 miles from the bomb site.

As I walked through the memorial, I was struck by the results of this community effort by people of the city. In the days after the bombing, we heard numerous accounts of how the people of the city were pulling together to restore some semblance of order. Local television stations requested donations of gloves, shovels, or baby clothes, and within minutes they returned to say, "We have enough. Please don't bring any more." Pastors, medical personnel, and social workers poured into the downtown area to help the survivors and families of the victims. Hundreds volunteered to donate blood and stood in line for hours to do so. News reports indicated that this kind of community spirit was unusual, but we saw it demonstrated time and again in the weeks after the bombing. Many people in Oklahoma City said they noticed softened interactions among people in the following weeks. It was almost as if we were all trying to be a little kinder to one another. In one suburb, signs along the road repeated the word "hope" for several miles. Volunteers who came from all over the world spoke of the resilient spirit of the people of Oklahoma City.

I don't know that we're any different from other cities. This kind of tragedy can bring a community effort in most places, as we saw in New York City after the terrorist destruction of the World Trade Towers. But we in Oklahoma City, and probably those in New York City, are proud of how ours responded. The Oklahoma City memorial commemorates not only the 168 people who died, the survivors, and their families but also the efforts of hundreds of volunteers who responded to the call to help.

For Reflection and Discussion

1. Nobody likes to talk about death and dying. Discuss how this topic was first introduced to you as a child? Do you think early experiences impacted you negatively or positively?

2. Why do you think that college students are intrigued with the author's Death and Dying class? Would you sign up for a class like this? Why or why not?

3. Many social scientists who have studied this topic state that death in the U.S. is a social problem. What do you think this means? Do you agree?

4. Why do you think we attempt to "deny death?"

5. In today's modern society, we relinquish the "work" of death to paid professionals. Though none of us would go back to a time when the family did all of these tasks, the author maintains that we may be missing something by not being intimately involved in these processes. What do you think?

6. Much of the care we provide for grieving families often occurs in the week surrounding a death and funeral. What are examples of long-term care that a community of faith could provide?

7. Though none of us is eager to return to the days when families "in mourning" were required to wear black, can you see how dressing in mourning clothes might actually be a healthful way to deal with grief?

8. What might be involved in a grief counseling workshop? Are you familiar with these services in your church or in your community? Do you we need to "learn how to grieve?"

9. Most congregations rely on the pastor or pastoral staff to deal with death and dying issues in the church. How could trained volunteers help with this process?

10. How is a death that results from a horrific event such as the Oklahoma City bombing or World Trade Center attack different from a "natural" death? How would you approach the victims' families differently?

PART 3

Communities That Transform Us

If we want to rebuild community, then we must build communities that transform us.

The word "transform" has an almost magical quality. It seems full of hope and promise of what could be possible. It assumes that the old is gone and the new version is improved. As Christians, we understand being transformed—the New Testament is full of illustrations of old changed into new.

My dictionary uses phrases like "to change in composition or structure; to change the outward form or appearance of; to change in character or condition." And my favorite from the field of electricity: "to change in potential."

If our families, neighborhoods, and churches are to be changed for the better, we will need transformation. If our goal is genuine community and "front porch" societies, we have a lot of work to do. It's time for us to take a realistic look at ways we can make this happen.

In Part 3 we get practical. Here we look at how to build front-porch communities. We look at communities that work, efforts around the country that are keeping us connected with each other. They're not all good, but they're not all bad either. Perhaps we can all find ways to be included in these new versions of community life. We just may be surprised to learn that there's hope in what some are calling *communities that transform us.*

8

Myths from Mayberry

*Since the Christian community is the living presence
of the mediating Christ, it enables us to be fully aware
of the painful condition of the human family
without being paralyzed by this awareness.*
—Henri Nouwen

*Let us not become weary in doing good, for
at the proper time we will reap a harvest if we
do not give up. Therefore, as we have opportunity,
let us do good to all people, especially to those
who belong to the family of believers.*
—Gal. 6:9-10

Otis, the town drunk, wanders into Mayberry's jail and
lets himself in to his own private cell.

The jail cell is reminiscent of a quaint bed and breakfast
inn, and here Otis sleeps off his drinking spell in the company of people who know and love him, assured that a warm
meal awaits him in the morning.

Aunt Bee, perpetually clad in her apron, her expansive
girth evidence of many good meals, lives only to serve Andy
and Opie, and she's always on hand to iron clothes or wash
windows or solve a problem at any hour of the day or night.
Her house is warm and welcoming, decorated with her
handiwork and numerous thriving plants. The big front
porch allows the whole family to sit and greet friends and
neighbors as they pass.

Andy and his deputy, Barney Fife, who have been dating
the same two "girls" for years, regularly visit Floyd's Barber

Shop to talk with the other men and catch up on the news. The two lawmen face personal problems or major issues of concern to the townspeople during each episode but always seem to resolve these dilemmas within the half hour—and all is well again in the community of Mayberry, North Carolina.

If you've watched any late night television lately, you've seen the classic shows like *The Andy Griffith Show.* And you may long for small-town life and for the good old days when life was simple—a community where everybody knew you and your family, where everybody waved or spoke to you as they walked down the street. It seemed that the neighbors would always lend a hand. This was a place where all worked together for the community's good.

If only we could have families, neighborhoods, and communities like those our grandparents had, or like those on television, life would be so simple, we feel.

In those days life's problems seemed simpler, too. None of the television programs dealt with serious issues such as child abuse, teen pregnancy, or divorce. They never focused on the problems we hear about every day when we turn on the television.

Current prime-time television programs routinely feature problems that were never mentioned in polite company in that simpler time. It's not that these problems didn't exist back then—they did. They just didn't show up on our television sets in our homes every day.

So it's easy to see why, as we look back, everything appears simpler. If only we could have families, neighborhoods, and communities like those our grandparents had, or like those on television, life would be so simple, we feel.

Everything seemed to be so much easier back then. Everybody worked hard, and at the end of the day, after a sumptuous meal that might include fresh green beans, corn, and tomatoes from the family garden, several generations would sit together on the front porch making homemade ice cream, eating gingersnaps, and greeting their neighbors and friends.

I hate to burst our bubbles, but most people's lives were not like those portrayed by *The Waltons, The Donna Reed Show,* or *Leave It to Beaver.* Yet we look to those television shows that depict the "good old days" and wish things could be that way again, or the way we like to think they were. We feel guilty because our lives don't seem to measure up to the ideal we've created.

It's not uncommon for us, thanks to CNN, to know more about what's happening on the other side of the planet than what's happening on the other side of the fence.

It's hard not to make these comparisons when many of us come home from work, push the automatic garage door opener, and disappear into our homes. We don't come out until the next morning, when we repeat the cycle by leaving through the garage, automatically closing the garage door, and barricading ourselves in our cars. We may wave to our neighbors, but we have no idea what their daily lives are like. We don't know their children's names or what pets they have, and we certainly don't have a clue about their problems.

It's not uncommon for us, thanks to CNN, to know more about what's happening on the other side of the planet than what's happening on the other side of the fence. We can watch events taking place live throughout the global village and yet know little about the events occurring in our local area.

For example, during the 2000 presidential elections in the United States (George W. Bush versus Al Gore), all the major networks declared one candidate the winner to later rescind their declarations. The news stories reflected the uncertainty of the events as they occurred. Throughout this process, the news anchors provided regular updates, analysis of the events, and presented positions for viewers to adopt their personal opinions.

While news reporting is a great service to help us keep in touch with events throughout the global village, do we sacrifice valuable personal involvement in the process? Do we abandon the human interaction we hold so dear by giving others the privilege of reporting on these human events? Does our lack of involvement glorify the role of "gossip" to a highly valued position—which devalues personal perspective, personal behavior, and personal responsibility for community events? Are we sacrificing the very human contact we say we long for?

Perhaps our greatest concerns are for our families. Today's families don't seem as close as those of the past, and our ancestors didn't seem to be stressed out over the serious, almost apocalyptic problems we live with today. We seem to be continuously reminded of the demise of the family structure, the death of the true American family.

We have abundant research studies and statistical reports comparing the families of today with those of the past. Usually today's families don't seem to measure up. But is this an accurate perspective? Are families today more fragile than in the past? Are our families living, as some have said, on the brink of disaster? The answer is not clear—it's both yes and no.

As much as we would like to believe that life was grand for our parents and grandparents, it just wasn't so.

In her books *The Way We Never Were* and *The Way We Really Are,* Stephanie Coontz sheds some light on our need to believe that the families of the past were better than today's, and on our apparent willingness to carry the guilt of not living the contented lives that we believe our ancestors did.

First of all, she points out that the "good old days" were not all that good. As much as we would like to believe that life was grand for our parents and grandparents, it just wasn't so. Even though at family gatherings our elderly relatives regale us with those warm stories of their families of the past and we all wish it could be so today, we may be kidding ourselves. And Grandma and Grandpa, though not intentionally, just may be leaving out some important parts of the saga.[1]

I realized this a few years ago when an elderly friend chastised the grandchildren for fighting with each other and talked of how well he got along with his brothers and sisters when they were children. To hear him tell the story, they were models of cooperation back in those days. Ironically, he wasn't speaking to two of his brothers and refused to visit in his sister's home, so apparently only in the good old days did they get along so well. I had to smile at this.

Coontz states that today's serious social problems are not new, nor are they more of a problem than in the past. Dilemmas such as child abuse, poverty, teen runaways, alcoholism, and drug addiction have been around for a while.

Child abuse, which is a serious concern today, has actually been a part of family life throughout American history; however, the abuse of the past was rarely considered the concern of any one outside the family. What happened behind closed doors has long been considered a private matter. And to make matters worse, a child or spouse who was beaten by a family member had little recourse. There was nowhere to go for help, no shelters to hide in or counselors to confide to, and relatives often could not or would not take the responsibility of another mouth to feed.

Among the English settlers in colonial times, brutal beatings of children by their parents were routine, and wives were commonly "taught a lesson" by their husbands, for both wives and children were legally the property of the husband/father and could be dealt with as he saw fit. This violent behavior of some early settlers was considered odd by many Native Americans, for they believed that striking a family member was pagan and immoral.

Later, as the English settlers traveled southwest, many Mexicans were also surprised at the settlers' use of violence as discipline for children and as punishment for convicted criminals, for both were foreign concepts.

Even today's poverty rate among children, though appalling with one of every five children living below the official poverty line, is not nearly as high as in the 1950s, when it was one of every three. Children ran away from home, became delinquent, and dropped out of school at alarming rates as late as the 1940s, when fewer than half of the young people who entered high school actually graduated.

If you speak with elderly relatives about their school experiences, few can tell you about attending their high school graduations—most didn't make it that far. Some can tell you, however, about the harsh discipline they received at school, about dropping out to join the army or get married, and the difficult economic situations in their families and communities.

This reality check doesn't have the same warm effect of Grandpa's good-old-days stories, and it doesn't look like a Hallmark commercial, but unfortunately it was true for much of the North American population until the mid 20th century.

We've all heard about the horrors of today's drug problems —it's almost a regular feature on news reports, in magazine and newspaper accounts, and it's the subject of numerous movies and television specials. We ask, "What can be done about today's youth and their serious drug problems? How can we stem the tide of illegal drugs entering our country?"

We already have a "drug czar" in Washington, D.C., overseeing the problem, and every school has a drug awareness program, for it is a serious *modern* problem—right? This is another myth.

Coontz points out that consumption of alcohol per capita was higher in the 1820s than it is today, and drug addiction (opium and cocaine) was epidemic throughout the United States population. Even many middle-class women were addicted to morphine and other powerful drugs.

We have no easy answers to today's family problems, but we never did in the first place.

During the mid 20th century, Valium was routinely prescribed for "nerves" for many middle-class adults and was probably one of the most abused prescription drugs.

Family research indicates that our new problems are really not so new after all. Thinking of them as long-term issues probably helps us to better understand them. According to Coontz, we have no easy answers to today's family problems, but we never did in the first place. She attempts to explain why we need to believe that things were better for our ancestors. "On both a personal and a social level, when things are going well, we credit our successful adherence to the family ideal, forgetting the conflicts, ambivalences and departures from the 'norm.' When things are going poorly, we look for the 'dysfunctional' elements of our family life, blaming our problems on 'abnormal' experiences or innovations."[2]

Rather than saying families are on the decline, it may be more accurate to say that families are changing. (But so is everything about our Western culture, where we value change as inevitable and necessary for improvement and success.) One thing we can know for sure: it is self-defeating to gaze longingly at the past and wish we could be transported back to the times of our elders, where we perceive life to have been simpler.

In *Family in Transition*, the editors discuss some of the most harmful myths about the family of the past and how these myths can affect us and our families today. As we examine our families, one myth is that of a "stable, harmonious past." This can be especially debilitating and result in guilty feelings for most of us, especially when we compare our families to an idealized image that's impossible to achieve. According to the editors, "Historians have found that premarital sexuality, illegitimacy, generational conflict, and even infanticide can best be studied as a part of family life itself rather than as separate categories of deviation."

They conclude that families have always had problems, and no "golden age" exists when all was well in the family. Throughout all of these problems, amazingly, the family as a social institution seems to have remained fairly resilient. The family has been able to adapt to the many social changes throughout the generations.[3]

For us to conclude . . . that our families are without hope is to ignore the resilient history of the family.

This is not to say, of course, that serious problems don't exist. As an example of the various problems families face, we can first consider the chapter titles of any book about family. Most current family textbooks highlight problems such as poverty, divorce, and violence within this intimate environment. Arlene and Jerome Skolnick, who have studied transitions in the family for 20 years, stress that, yes, today's families have their challenges, but most of these challenges are old ones. They point out that one of the best ways to gauge this is to look at reports from literature and through other media messages such as radio and television. "From the

Bible to the fairy tale, from Sophocles to Shakespeare, from Eugene O'Neill to the soap opera, there is a tragic tradition of portraying the family as a 'high-voltage emotional setting, charged with love and hate, tenderness and spite, even incest and murder.'"

Many family sitcoms have taken a humorous look at the crisis events that occur within families. While some critics complain that these programs present a less-than-realistic (or too realistic) view of family life, and in some cases solutions that are less than ideal, they do show families grappling with problems that many viewers can relate to. This is in contrast to most sitcoms of the past, which glossed over family turmoil and portrayed the family as a setting of perpetual contentment.

Even on nearly every episode of _The Simpsons_, where parents and children may not be the best role models, the family ends up doing what most of us would consider right, and the children learn a lesson in the process. Does the language and behavior portrayed by the characters overshadow the lesson? You be the judge.

For us to conclude, however, that our families are without hope is to ignore the resilient history of the family. Families of the past were not always settings of harmony. As we attempt to build "front porch" families today, it's helpful to keep this healthy historical perspective. _The Andy Griffith Show_ was a classic television show and continues to entertain viewers today, but it's only a story on television and is probably not the best guide for how families should live today. And it's self-defeating to gaze longingly at the past. Mayberry was a wonderful place to visit, but we can't (and we probably don't want) to live there.

We should focus on the encouraging message seen in the resilience of the family to adapt to change. It's actually encouraging to realize that the family, which we as Christians believe is ordained by God, is a dynamic social institution and according to the best research, will continue to evolve. But it's here to stay.

For Reflection and Discussion

1. From classic sitcoms, what are some of the myths we have come to believe about life in the "good old days?" Does any one program appear more realistic than the others?

2. We're sometimes disappointed to learn that the classic television shows didn't reflect the real lives of the actors or the lives of most people who watched. Why do we want to hold on to these myths? What do they provide for us?

3. What are the dangers of destroying the myths of the family past? Do we do ourselves a disservice?

4. Does the news media tell us too much? Do you think they have a hidden agenda in the way they report the news?

5. Skolnick and Skolnick and Coontz provide a reality check for us by telling us what wasn't so good about the "good old days." From talking with older relatives, what can you add to the list?

6. Coontz says there are no easy answers to today's problems, but there never were. How can we improve our approach to "fixing the family" by understanding the family in historical context?

7. What are some examples of how today's families are resilient? Is it more accurate to say that families are simply changing rather than on the decline?

8. What are some of the unique challenges for people of faith as they seek to improve family life and disregard the myths?

9. Give some examples of strategies your family (or a family you know of) uses to build genuine community. What does your family do at holidays that encourages a feeling of connectedness?

10. Finally, what do you want to take with you from your family of origin, and what do (did) you want to leave behind in establishing your own family?

9

A Church Under
a Bridge

*Community is not a place or a thing;
it is a calling, a struggle, a journey.*
—Robert Booth Fowler

You may . . . come to share in the very being of God.
—2 Pet. 1:4

One of the best places to worship God on a Sunday
morning is the "Church Under the Bridge" in Waco,
Texas. Yes, they truly worship under a bridge, and of course
everyone asks, "Why would they want to do that?"

This church is the brainstorm of Jimmy and Janet Dor-
rell. Twenty years ago they brought their young family to
live in an area of run-down houses and high crime rates,
where their neighbors include prostitutes, drug dealers, the
poor, and the homeless. Unlike many who give a few years
to an inner-city ministry, Jimmy and Janet have made it their
life. They are a part of the community.

For many years Mission Waco, a ministry of the church,
has conducted "poverty simulations," introducing affluent
youth to a weekend of homelessness. They can hardly keep
up with the demand of young people wanting to sign up for
this experience. The students arrive on Friday night, and immediately their possessions are taken away, except for two
items they can keep with them for the weekend. They spend
the rest of the weekend fending for themselves, "Dumpster

diving" for food and sleeping outside. (And they actually *pay* for this experience!)

Seldom does anybody leave on Sunday unchanged. Jimmy says, "It's kind of like a Slinky—every time you take it out, it stretches a little bit and doesn't fit in the box quite like it used to."

Another Mission Waco experiment is the Ark, a diverse population of 25 formerly homeless people who live in a unique housing arrangement, an apartment complex unlike any other. They not only live in the same complex but also have to be accountable to each other. They meet regularly and are "required to care" about each other in order to live in the low-rent community. It works and is changing lives.

The Dorrells started having Sunday morning services under the highway overpass to meet the needs of a few homeless persons who didn't feel comfortable sitting in a church on a pew. Now hundreds of people meet there every week, and the services are glorious.

Looking at the success of Mission Waco, I have to ask, "What makes a good community?"

How will we know it when we see it? Can we improve on the faith communities we already have?

Perhaps what makes the Waco community unique is that it's "designed for sharing." In the 20 years since Jimmy and Janet came to Waco, they have often stumbled, sometimes fallen, and occasionally triumphed. They have reorganized and reworked their dream. And with the help of volunteers, they continue to grow in their ability to be a community. The key just may be their belief that they're supposed to be a community; they're designed to live and share in community with other believers. They're convinced that they need each other in order to make community happen.

Reuben Welch, a former college chaplain, wrote a powerful book titled *We Really Do Need Each Other.* Welch is convinced that a community of believers must depend on each other and help each other out in times of need. He seems to think this is a requirement of those in a community of faith. In his final chapter he writes that as a people of faith, we *have* to depend on others in order to make it: "You know some-thing—we're all just people who need each other. We're all learning, and we've all got a long journey ahead of us. We've got to go together, and if it takes till Jesus comes, we better stay together, we better help each other. . . . Because that's how it is in the body of Christ."[1]

The challenge for the rest of us may be to examine the communities of faith in which we live and see what we can do to make them into genuine caring communities— places where we really do need each other, depend on each other, and strive to build each other.

Of course, not everyone can live in a highly unorthodox inner-city faith community like Mission Waco with its daily emphasis on being "in community" and needing each other.

Let's be realistic—not everyone can take on the tasks that the Dorrells have. The challenge for the rest of us may be to examine the communities of faith in which we live and see what we can do to make them into genuine caring commu-nities—places where we really do need each other, depend on each other, and strive to build each other, thereby build-ing true community in which success is measured in changed environments and changed lives.

How do we approach this task? First of all, we must ask ourselves if this is truly what we want. Do we really want to be in fellowship with our fellow believers? Looking around, do we even like these people? OK, sometimes we don't like each other very much, especially when we disagree. But those minor skirmishes set aside, do we truly desire to live in community with other believers?

When I was in college, I attended a church that welcomed students from local colleges and provided them with meals, programs, and a marvelous Sunday School teacher. I don't know how we got so lucky to have Bob Benson as our teacher for a few years, but I was fortunate enough to be at the right school at just the right time. Bob taught this gigantic group of skeptical 18- to 22-year-olds who questioned everything.

Before his untimely death, Bob wrote several books, including what I think is one of his best: *Come Share the Being.* The title is from 2 Pet. 1:4 "You may . . . come to share in the very being of God" (NEB). Bob had a rare gift of being able to take profound theological principles, present them in their most basic form, and teach college students a valuable lesson in the process. Over several years, he convinced most of us that one of the most important characteristics of a faith community was that it was a community of sharing.

Now, we weren't completely open to this idea. Our generation lived through Vietnam, Kent State, and Watergate. We didn't trust our parents or the government, and sometimes we didn't trust the Church. We felt our parents' generation had messed things up, and we were determined to do it better. So along comes Bob Benson with his quiet voice, gentle manner, and earth-shattering ideas. He said we would have to depend on each other, trust each other, and put aside our pride if we wanted to build a better community. He said it was actually a part of God's plan for us.

One story he told in class was about a church picnic. Most of us have been to these dinners in which everybody brings food and puts it all together for a collective meal. Bob used this story to theorize that in a true community of believers you could come to one of these picnics with a meager contribution—even a simple baloney sandwich wrapped up in brown paper—and others who had prepared an elaborate feast would welcome you anyway. . . . "And they spread it all out

beside you, and there you were with your baloney sandwich.
But they said to you, "Why don't we put it all together?"

"No, I couldn't do that, I just couldn't even think of it,"
you murmured embarrassedly.

"Oh, come on, there's plenty of chicken and pie and
everything—and we just love baloney sandwiches. Let's just
put it all together."

"And so you did and there you sat—eating like a king
when you came like a pauper."[2]

This is the kind of Christian community Bob talked
about in our Sunday School class—a community that values
every member, no matter how large or small his or her contribution. As we listened, we all wondered, *Is he serious?*

We all remembered the day he passed around a little
smooth stone and insisted that each one of us, all 75 of us,
feel it. It was just a little item he thought was a thing of
beauty and wanted to share with us.

We were used to these funky object lessons, but what
was this about "coming as you are" and "bringing whatever
you have to the table"? Did God really plan for us to need
each other, to overlook each other's faults and share what we
have with everybody else? Bob seemed to be saying that this
community-living idea was a requirement for God's people:
we're *supposed* to live in community.

**Could God have designed us to need other people?
Could He have made us in such a way that in order to
be a Christian and to share in His very being, we would
have to share in the community of others?**

You know, it *is* possible for homo sapiens to live on their
own. It *is* possible to move to the mountains or to a deserted
island and rarely, if ever, come into contact with other people.

What's interesting, however, is that throughout human history most of us have sought to be a part of a group, large or small. Most of us seek community. Could God have designed us to need other people? Could He have made us in such a way that in order to be a Christian and to share in His very being, we would have to share in the community of others? Well, Bob certainly thought so, and I've come to believe it as well.

Bob seemed to be saying that in order to be a person of faith and live in community with other people of faith, we have to admit that we can't do it all on our own. Unfortunately, this involves being vulnerable. It also involves serving others, being available to them, inconveniencing ourselves for them, and sometimes just putting our own desires on a shelf for a while. Bob was trying to get us to see that if we really wanted to be a part of the fellowship of believers, it would cost us something.

Well, we didn't immediately throw down our fishing nets and follow Bob. Sure, we were in favor of this New Testament living, but we didn't want to be uncomfortable in the process.

In 1985 sociologist Robert Bellah and his associates published a remarkable book titled *Habits of the Heart: Individualism and Commitment in American Life.* This same team of writers expanded its basic premise a few years later with *The Good Society.* These books received wide acclaim. In university settings, scholarly papers were written, classes were taught, book reports were researched, and conferences were convened focusing on the ideas in these books.

I recently heard Bellah speak at a workshop. I wasn't surprised that this man of 78, only recently "sort of" retired, was extremely self-deprecating and a little shy in the large group—many authors are. During that workshop, he presented a series of lectures on the topic of community and fielded questions. He spoke of the changes in North American society that make it difficult to build healthy communities. He spoke of the personal and collective barriers that keep us from caring about each other. He was especially critical of modern institutions that govern our lives and seem intent on keeping us isolated from each other. He spoke of a "radical individualism" that's encouraged by the culture in which we live.

Being a part of God's kingdom is not just having a private relationship with God but also having a communal relationship with His other children.

He was also critical of many churches that encourage "private piety" or a "just Jesus and me" approach to Christianity. Attempting to disassociate themselves from the organized church, some Christians even claim, "I'm not religious, but I'm very spiritual."

Bellah maintained that we need a tangible sense of the Church and that being a part of God's kingdom is not just having a private relationship with God but also having a communal relationship with His other children. Bellah's research points to the breakdown of commitments to others and to organized groups as contributing factors to what some call "an epidemic of loneliness and feelings of disconnectedness."

In other words, like Bob Benson, Bellah is saying we need each other—we need our families, we need our churches, and we need our neighborhoods.

One thing is certain: in our postmodern and post-Christian era, it isn't popular to say we need each other. In our age of individualism and personal gratification, we're told we can do it all on our own.

Research continues to indicate, however, that we lead healthier and happier lives when we're "connected" in meaningful relationships with those around us. And if we people of faith believe that God indeed designed us for fellowship with other Christians, our task is to find ways to build genuine settings in which this can take place. If, as Bob Benson would say, the Christian life is a shared life, then our job is to make it a reality.

For Reflection and Discussion:

1. Maybe some people want to have church under a bridge, but what about the rest of us? Some of us like our comfortable pews and climate-controlled sanctuaries. Is anything really wrong with that?

2. Isn't God glorified when we build elaborate sanctuaries in His name? What does the New Testament advise on this subject?

3. What are the dangers of getting caught up in beautiful buildings, opulent surroundings, and fellowship with people who look like us?

4. What are some specific ways we can "come to share in the very being of God?"

5. Regarding Bob Benson's church picnic story, is it actually possible to value every member, no matter how large or small his or her contribution?

6. Throughout history, most of us have sought community— to help us meet not just our physical needs but also our emotional and spiritual needs. What are some examples of our seeking community?

7. Robert Bellah has criticized the "private piety" or "just Jesus and me" approach to Christianity. Discuss the writing of others who admonished us to join with other believers.

8. Bellah maintains that being a part of God's kingdom is not just a private relationship with God but also a communal relationship with His other children. Is he saying it is impossible to be a Christian on your own, without being in a Christian community? Do you agree?

9. Bellah referred to an "epidemic of loneliness and feelings of disconnectedness" in our society. What examples of this have you observed?

10. What does it mean to say we are living in a "postmodern" and "post-Christian" era?

10

Living in an Upside-down World

We must become the change we want to see.
—Mahatma Gandhi

*Carry each other's burdens, and in this way
you will fulfill the law of Christ.*
—Gal. 6:2

Fast food is a sin! At least that's what a Catholic bishop in Italy maintained when he condemned McDonald's restaurants for serving less-than-nutritious food in a society known for long, leisurely family meals. He felt that waiting in line for an individual meal served in an individual container and rapidly consuming it—even in others' company—goes against the sanctity of community life and the spiritual experience of sharing a meal. Since fast-food restaurants, like McDonald's, encourage each family member to order what he or she wants, even if they do eat together, he claimed they are not actually "sharing a meal." The Italian bishop railed against the loss of community that results.

Not unlike the bishop, we must acknowledge that we're living in an upside-down world.

The beliefs we have as Christians, the hopes we have for our families, and the values we hold dear seem at times to be completely at odds with the world around us. My pastor used to talk about our being a "peculiar people"—standing out from the rest of the world, being set apart, different. In today's world most of us don't want to stand out to the extent that we're seen as peculiar. It sounds better to say we want to be "in the world but not of the world." We want to live in the postmodern world, but we don't want to be too different from it. Do we?

So how are we to live in this upside-down world and not be of this world? How are we to be upright in a world that seems upside down? How are we to live simple, faithful lives in our families, neighborhoods, and churches—lives that allow for front-porch conversations and front-porch fellowship?

We all know of religious groups that are out of step with the mainstream culture in terms of how they dress, worship, and live. Some Christians are not so sure they want to be considered that extreme. They do want to fit in. And they want their Christian lifestyle to be appealing to others.

When we ask someone if he or she wants to be a Christian, we're really asking if he or she wants to be like us. The way we live should be a good advertisement for the Christian walk.

When asked about their beliefs, some Christians begin with a list of all the things they're against, and to make matters worse, they seem to be against just about everything. And they're often hostile about it. These folks may sincerely believe they're living radical Christian lives, but no one wants to join anything that looks that dreadful. They appear *too* "peculiar."

A good bit of advice here is to remember that when we ask someone if he or she wants to be a Christian, we're really asking if he or she wants to be like us. The way we live should be a good advertisement for the Christian walk. Though being a Christian may cost us universal acceptance in many respects, should it also be appealing to others? Can it be both?

Perhaps we need to emphasize the joy of living in Christ, the change He has made in our lives, and the peace He provides for us. We should stress the hope that Christ brings, not the list of things we're missing out on because we've decided to be Christians.

Of course, there _are_ things we forgo in order to live a Christian life: for instance, my church denomination has always emphasized a Christian life without drinking and tobacco use. Even before the surgeon general warned us about the health risks, we (and other religious groups) took a stand against alcohol and tobacco. It's not always been a popular stance, and we've been out of step with the mainstream (if somewhat ahead of our time) on these issues.

Only in the last 25 years has the scientific community fully understood the risks of smoking and secondhand smoke. Today we know cigarette smoking kills far more people than many other serious health risks combined. So being "peculiar" all those years has paid off, at least in this case.

But our challenge is to build families, neighborhoods, and churches that are appealing and community oriented— living spaces that are inviting and welcoming. How, then, can we accomplish this?

Guideline 1: Design for Community

Perhaps the best place to start is to plan with community as one of the top priorities. Some of the most exciting examples of this are occurring in new, planned communities being built from the ground up. Some of these have houses with front porches facing each other and sharing a front yard. These neighborhoods have sidewalks (missing from many subdivisions built in the last 20 years) that encourage walking and, therefore, interacting with others. Indoor and outdoor community living areas are set aside for the families in the area to have picnics, parties, and recreational events. Some have outlawed fences between the homes, again encouraging neighbors to know each other and to be involved in each other's lives.

In other words, these new communities are designed around the theme of *community* instead of privacy and isolation.

Some of this may not be too appealing to those who value their privacy and enjoy *not* knowing their neighbors. Never fear—our private retreats are probably not in too much danger of disappearing entirely. But if we say we desire community and lament the loss of human interaction in modern society, then the architecture of the future will need to be designed to encourage shared living spaces.

One of the most dramatic examples of how architecture affects our daily living occurred in our neighborhood a few years ago after a particularly bad thunderstorm. The winds were nearly 80 miles per hour that night, and the next day fences had been blown down all over the city. In our area, most of our houses have a seven-foot stockade wood fence around back yards to keep our dog and the children in and to keep the neighbor's dog and children out.

In some large congregations there seems to be an abundance of gifts, football tickets, trips, new cars, and even cash bestowed on the pastor and his or her family while some families in the congregation live from paycheck to paycheck and can barely make ends meet.

Surprisingly, when these fences came down, some of us got to know our next-door neighbors for the first time. It was fascinating to watch people who had waved to each other for years now working together to rebuild their fences. People told me they had conversations with their neighbors for the first time in six years and realized that they actually had a lot in common. Others told me that when the fences went back up, they seldom spoke again and went back to waving from the front driveway as one or the other came or went.

Our churches can also be built to encourage community and interaction with others as we create opportunities for involvement that encourage a feeling of belonging. I'm saddened to hear pastors describe their congregation as one big, happy family, when often many within the congregation are unable to feel a sense of belonging. In some large congregations there seems to be an abundance of gifts, football tickets, trips, new cars, and even cash bestowed on the pastor and his or her family while some families in the congregation live from paycheck to paycheck and can barely make ends meet.

A few years ago, a visiting pastor at our church spent much of his sermon talking about his sports car hobby and collection. It was hard to pay attention, for I knew many young people in the sanctuary that day were wondering where they would find the money to put gas in their used car that week. It's not enough to pray for God to meet the needs of those within our community. He expects us, as people of faith, to do something about those needs.

Next we have to take into account that our communities, and even our definitions of community, have changed since our parents' and grandparents' day. With the rapid technological advances in our world, an increasing number of ways to communicate, and electronic communities often taking the place of old-fashioned front porches, it's probably unrealistic to hang on to the myths of the "good old days." It's likely that our society will become even more complex, so longing for romanticized versions of the past is probably unproductive. What can we do with the world we have? How can we make it more "human"?

Guideline 2: Slow Down Our Lives

One reason we lead such fast-paced lives is because we *can*. The sophisticated technology that's a characteristic of living in a postmodern age allows us to fill our days with "multitasking"—doing several things at once. We can check our stock portfolio, send an E-mail message, listen to a great new compact disk, and talk to Mom while barreling down the highway at 75 miles an hour. Our hand-held computers can keep us on schedule, remind us of birthdays, and measure our body fat all at the same time.

We think nothing of commuting an hour or more to work, and we fill that time by returning telephone calls, writing reports, or playing solitaire. Our ancestors would have said that's too far to travel, that two hours of travel time every day is too much. It may have been for them, but not for us. We try to fit everything we possibly can into the time we have. As a result, we just may be doing ourselves and our families a disservice.

"Just saying no" won't work for all of us, either. Many of us, as people of faith, have chosen to serve in our churches and in our communities. When the news gets out that we're willing and able to help, you can bet we'll be called upon. We can't say no to the worthwhile projects that come our way or to the important family events and gatherings, and, well, we can't say no to everything, can we?

As simplistic as it sounds, the lesson is that we can slow down our lives by saying no to some "opportunities for service" and by being selective when we do say yes.

So how are we to slow down our modern lives *and* serve those around us? How can we help build a sense of community again and slow down our lives at the same time?

The answer may be "selective service," a personal system

of carefully choosing the programs, activities, and events in which we'll participate. In high school and college, I was afflicted with the "join everything and be the leader" malady. I don't know how I ever had time to get homework finished and keep my decent grade point average—too much was happening at school, and I didn't want to miss any of it. I seemed to believe that if it was going to get done, *I* had to be the one to do it—especially if it was going to be done right!

As you might imagine, I got in over my head, and I see students today doing the same thing. In the midst of this, I received some good advice from an older friend in the church whom I greatly respected. He said one way of looking at it was this: if I took on all the jobs in the church, that might actually prevent someone else from being able to serve—someone who might be waiting to be asked to participate.

Now, I don't know if he was just trying to convince me to slow down or was warning me of the dangers of overcommitting and burning out, but it worked. After our discussion, I felt free to say no without guilt, knowing that someone else would take on the task and might even do a better job of it. It was a liberating experience.

As simplistic as it sounds, the lesson is that we can slow down our lives by saying no to some "opportunities for service" and by being selective when we do say yes. We may also be able to simplify our worlds by limiting the technological "conveniences" we "need"—conveniences that are becoming more and more affordable yet often isolate us from those around us. We can take positive steps toward building community by spending time with the people who are dearest to us—friends and families. Try it—you'll be surprised.

Guideline 3: Plan for a "Community.com" World

The cyberfreaks and webmasters among us are not the only ones we will need to embrace in our ever-changing, postmodern world. We may actually have to accept different definitions of community. People are still talking to each other—they're communicating, getting in touch. What's different is how this is happening.

And what we have before us may in some ways be an improvement. Young adults away from home for the first time are communicating with their parents more than ever before. College students who have little to say on the phone and would never write a letter actually share their daily lives, and sometimes their innermost feelings, with their parents via E-mail.

My students frequently tell me about electronic conversations they have with their parents. These are parents who previously tried in vain to get details out of their college son or daughter and got only monosyllabic grunts or a short answer to their questions. These parents are now delighted to actually "talk" by E-mail with their offspring—the same ones they keep sending those checks to every month. Students are "talking" daily with their parents and actually revealing feelings and struggles. You have to admit—this is an improvement, even for the kids, because they now have a much faster and direct means of hitting up Mom and Dad for money. This is one of the new forms of community, one of the new definitions of community life.

In addition, old friends and family members who have been out of touch for years are now sitting at a computer and communicating with each other. Relationships are being restored and new ones formed. Baron says this is partially due to the novelty of the Internet and the speed with which we can interact, but it also has something to do with being less threatening. Because the rules for grammar and spelling are more relaxed in E-mail messages, there's more freedom. Also, Baron says that once we master Internet messaging, most of us, young and old, enjoy the process—it's more fun than handwriting a letter and less intimidating than a telephone call. She views this as one of the many advantages of our technological revolution, and she's right.

Next, we have to realize that things are seldom as bad as we think they are or as bad as we're told. The lack of community may not be of disastrous proportions.

Guideline 4: Consider the Least of These

It happened again last night. Another person died on the street in my city. This was not the result of crime or of a car accident, but because of hunger and exposure to the below-freezing temperature. It's ridiculous, I'm told, considering that publicly funded housing is available to these people. Rescue missions and city shelters are numerous throughout the downtown area. Something like this should never happen, others say. And they're right—it should never happen.

Visitors from Japan are often shocked at the poverty they see when they come to the United States. They come here expecting to find a land of plenty where everyone is wealthy and prosperous. They're aware of the crime rate, and many even take classes beforehand to prepare—one class is called "How to Visit the U.S. and Stay Alive."

But what they often find surprising is the number of people sleeping on the street and how frequently they are approached in large, urban areas and asked for handouts. It's hard for them to understand how the richest, most powerful nation on the planet can live with such extremes. It's hard for the rest of us to understand too.

Whatever our political leanings may be or however our interpretations of the many scriptures concerning the poor differ, one thing is certain: we can't hold "the least of these" in contempt.

Of course, I'm told that some of them *want* to live on the street. I'm told that some homeless people commit a crime just to be put in jail and thus receive a warm bed and a decent meal. People tell me, as if to justify the situation, that the poor really want to live that way and we shouldn't feel bad about it. After all, we pay our taxes and the government —not we—should be doing something about it.

What bothers me most about these statements is that they're often said with contempt. Whatever our political leanings may be or however our interpretations of the many scriptures concerning the poor differ, one thing is certain: we can't hold "the least of these" in contempt. This I'm fairly sure about, and that's perhaps the hardest part for all of us.

Most of us have what's called "compassion fatigue." Even though we're concerned about the social problems around us and think something needs to be done, we don't know how to go about it. And in our litigious society, we're afraid of doing the wrong thing and perhaps being sued. And then there's the dirt factor. If we're to love these people as Christ loved them and welcome them into our churches, things are going to get messed up.

I was on the front lines of the bus ministry at our church, and let me tell you—it was messy! Some of those little kids we picked up on our bus route were filthy and had no idea of how to behave in church. They ran, yelled, punched, and kicked, although the regular church kids also did their share. The bus-route kids offered challenges to be met, and many church members were not so sure it was worth all the trouble. These "outsiders" were perhaps more than we had bargained for. Surely this is not what Jesus meant when he said "go into all the world." It seemed a whole lot easier to just write a check and send it to the mission field far, far away.

What if Jesus was truly the leader of our congregation? What if He were our pastor? One of the first things He might require is that we redirect our energies. Instead of being a community in which everybody looks like us, Jesus might call on us to diversify, to embrace those of other nationalities, races, cultures, economic levels, and political persuasions. It would be more than most of us could stand— our churches would never be the same. What a radical idea!

Guideline 5: Don't Isolate Yourself

Of course, this is much easier said than done in a society that provides us with too many opportunities to facilitate isolation. It's not always easy to trust each other—in families, in neighborhoods, even in our communities of faith. Talk to anyone who has been hurt in one of these settings, and they can tell you about having the wind knocked out of them when they felt betrayed by someone they trusted. Without a doubt, it's difficult and scary to put ourselves on the line and risk being hurt by those we care about most. We're tempted to withdraw and to avoid hurt by avoiding relationships. This works for only a few of us. The rest of us "really do need each other," and our lives are fuller because of close re-lationships.

There's a new feature in the newspaper I read every day—a regular column on how to get along with the people at work. Actually, it often focuses on how to get your work done _in spite of_ the people at work. This isn't really a new concept, I guess. Many of the letters to Ann Landers and Dear Abby are about workplace conflict, and the "Dilbert" comic strip deals with the "turkeys" we have to put up with at work. It's scary how we can all relate to these letters and cartoons.

This is not unlike the conflicts we experience in our families. Perhaps there are extended families somewhere who can get together and actually spend more than 24 hours without conflict, but research indicates that they're rare. Family therapists are busy before every holiday, prepar-ing their clients to get along with their families and repair-ing the wounds of that inevitable conflict. Some theorists maintain that the close emotional bonds and shared histories within families lead to this conflict and that some disagree-ment is unavoidable.

Perhaps we should make the best of our work situations, accepting the fact that we're unlikely to like and be liked by everyone. I'm fairly certain that God doesn't require that we

agree with all our family members either. We may have to
accept that being in community with others, even others we
don't get along with, is not too much to ask, and isolating
ourselves—at work or within family life—is probably not
the answer, though we could probably be excused for skip-
ping some family reunions and a few workplace potlucks.

**We were never meant to isolate ourselves and focus
on own personal journey and spend all our time
building up our own walk. The New Testament says
to become a Christian and then get to work.**

Guideline 6: Seek Inclusive Communities

In recent years many Christian groups have emphasized
strengthening our individual spiritual lives. Many in the
church have benefited from valuable activities such as personal journaling, joining prayer groups, and participating in
Bible studies. Not surprisingly, a huge industry has grown up
around our need to draw closer to God through personal
prayer and Bible reading. You can now purchase complete
kits with study materials, workbooks, and exercises for individual spiritual growth. Some even have a money-back
guarantee: "Your prayer life will improve or your money
back." Especially for new Christians, what could be better
than step-by-step directions for growing in one's personal
Christian walk?

The problem may be that the Christian walk was never
meant to be individual. We were never meant to isolate ourselves and focus on our own personal journey and spend all
our time building up our own walk. The New Testament
says to become a Christian and then *get to work*. Maybe we're
not supposed to sit around contemplating our own spiritual
navels. Maybe we're supposed to get beyond our church
walls and help those around us—whether they attend our

church or not. Perhaps the scriptures are telling us to go beyond the Bible studies and do something about the social
problems in our communities. Instead of praying a little (and
eating a lot) at the men's prayer breakfast, maybe we're supposed to get to know those rough kids down the street from
the church, maybe even open the church gym to them.

Recently I did some consulting with a large metropoli-
tan church on the East Coast whose members were reaching
out to the people living around the church—an area that has
evolved during the 75 years that the church has been at this
location. Once the members of the church lived within
walking distance; today most commute from the outlying
residential communities. The church members (1000+) are
predominantly white middle-class, and the surrounding
community is a racially mixed, mostly low-income area. I
met with a small group of volunteers from the church who
wanted to do something to help the people who lived near-
by and wanted to make their church a more welcoming
place. I was impressed with their concern and their willingness to change the community image of their congregation.

Their first task was to conduct a community audit. On a
cold winter Sunday morning, 100 volunteers went door-to-
door asking people about their lives and about their views of
the community. Without identifying themselves as being
from the church, they asked about the best and worst characteristics in the area. They asked about immediate family
needs and about what needed to be done long-term in the
neighborhood. Finally, they asked for suggestions for classes
or services that could be offered by the local churches. What
they found in the surveys was shocking.

Within the shadow of this thriving church, the volunteers
found people who asked only that their heat or electricity to
be turned back on. One person asked for soap, and another
wanted grocery money. Of course, more abstract requests and
spiritual concerns were expressed as well, and many volun-

teers were surprised to find people who wanted them to just stay and talk. The volunteers met afterward to discuss what they could do as a congregation. They found it unsettling that people living in houses and apartments they drove by each week on their way to Sunday services had such needs. The volunteers expressed their shock and shame—and then they got to work. They bought groceries, paid utility bills, and looked at concrete ways that people in their wealthy congregation could impact the community. They began to offer computer classes, open their recreational facilities, and make their church building more community friendly.

The same church that for many years emphasized members building their personal growth and had an exclusive reputation in the community began to seek ways to live the New Testament challenge to be inclusive. They are beginning to see beyond the needs of their own congregation and are starting to change the community around them.

Guideline 7: Meet Crisis Needs

One advantage of growing up in a small rural church in the 1950s was getting to experience a missionary ladies' bandage roll. If you've never seen one of these, you don't know what you're missing. The ladies of our church would gather monthly to talk about the needs of the missionaries in far-off lands, pray for them by name, and of course, eat. I remember my mom tearing up old white bed linens to take to the bandage roll, and I listened to the stories she would tell afterward. Apparently there was a great need for bandages in Africa, and a call went out to church ladies in North America for clean strips of cotton sheets to be rolled and shipped overseas.

Before we can meet the needs of people within the walls of the church, in the shadow of the church, or on the mission field, we have to understand the needs. This is one of the many ways that technological advances can help the church keep up-to-date on the needs around us. We have no excuse for being ignorant of the community's needs when information and the latest statistics are at our fingertips via our computers. We can find out current data about that re-mote New Guinea village or the needs of people who live across the street from the church. We can compile, organize, and analyze this information quickly and put it to work where the needs are greatest. There are people in our churches (also known as cyberfreaks and webmasters) who can use their skills to aid the Kingdom. What a way to build community!

Guideline 8: Avoid Counterfeit Designs

We're told that more than 80 percent of the things we worry about never come about. Many of us spend our time contemplating what we will do _if_, and the _if_ never happens. Barry Glassner in _The Culture of Fear: Why Americans Are Afraid of the Wrong Things_ emphasizes that many of our fears are unfounded: "Give us a happy ending and we write a dis-aster story. . . . The more things improve, the more pessimis-tic we become."[1]

As we moved into the year 2000, the crime rate was down, the number of drug users was down, the unemploy-ment rate was down, and we were healthier than ever be-fore. Yet many North Americans (more than half) believed just the opposite.

For many years we've known that people who watch a lot of television are more likely to have unrealistic fears. They are more likely to fear being a victim of family break-up, violent crime, a natural disaster, or even a "flesh-eating virus."

These unusual events take place on the tube far more frequently than they do in real life. It's interesting that mid-dle-aged white women are the least likely to be victims of stranger assault, yet they are often the ones who fear it most.

If we watch the local news, we may all believe that any day the world will explode around us.

In my area, where three television stations compete for a limited number of hard news stories, the motto seems to be "If it bleeds, it leads." On slow news days (and we seem to have a lot of these) we are even told of disasters that *almost* happened in our town. "Tune in at 6:00 to hear if a horde of locusts is headed toward your subdivision!" Now, don't you think that if that horde were actually coming our way, we shouldn't have to wait until 6:00 to hear about it? Who are they kidding?

A journalist friend of mine says, "We should never believe everything we hear or read, but with all our hearts we should believe everything we say or write." It seems that each week I hear some preposterous story or receive an E-mail message that predicts impending doom unless I immediately send it on to six of my closest friends and send a dollar to the original writer. Obviously some people have a lot of time on their hands and a lot of extra cash lying around.

A speaker recently related this story to illustrate how hungry people are to be a part of a community effort. A disc jockey on a popular Dallas radio station asked each of his listeners to send in $20. He never told them what his plans were for the money. In the next few weeks, he received $42,000 in the mail. The speaker who told this story was sure that this was evidence that the listening public wanted to be a part of something, even if they didn't know what the money was being collected for. Maybe that was the motivation, but I'm wondering if it just proves how gullible some of us are. By the way, the shocked disc jockey donated the money to charity.

Our modern society has no shortage of predictions of doom and gloom, and an overabundance of counterfeit designs for how we should live. The lesson here seems to be for each of us to sift the good news and the bad and to draw our conclusions with the help of enduring biblical guidelines and trusted advisers. As we seek to shed light on "crises" bombarding us daily, we can find no better filters than these.

For Reflection and Discussion

1. What are some examples of trying to live upright in an upside-down world?

2. The author provides eight guidelines for community building and some strategies for making community happen. How does each one link with one of chapters 1-8?

3. "Designing for community" sounds expensive, but does it have to be? What changes can be made in your community of faith that won't cost anything?

4. As our world continues to change, one of our greatest challenges may be to acknowledge new definitions for community. How can we embrace the new technologies without losing the human touch?

5. Do you think we live in a "culture of fear?" Why do we overestimate some dangers and underestimate others? Are we afraid of the wrong things?

6. Provide some examples of individuals or groups who have isolated themselves from modern society. How did they do it, and what concessions have they made, if any?

7. It's easy to say we need to simplify our lives and slow down. But this is hard to do. What steps can we take toward making this happen?

8. Although you recognize the seriousness of social problems such as child abuse and neglect, you may have "compassion fatigue." What are some ways we as the community of faith can collectively tackle one or more of these concerns? What could your group do?

9. In recent years Christian groups have expressed a desire for racial reconciliation, but we still seem to be segregated, especially in our churches. Is it hopeless?

10. Nothing indicates the extent to which a faith group believes in community like its response to a crisis (inside or outside its walls). Besides a death in the family, what are some other crisis events that require the community of faith to "move into action?"

<u>Conclusion</u>
Truly Transformed Communities

Our attempts at community building may at times be exhilarating, but they may also be exhausting. Anyone who has attempted to change his or her surroundings for the better has experienced discouragement, disillusionment, and disagreement. Rebuilding community in our isolated worlds won't be easy. And it may at times be messy work.

But if we're to be "truly transformed," it will be because of the efforts of those among us who believe we can all become better—as individuals and as a culture—by reconciling with, forgiving, assisting, and believing in each other, and by giving each other the benefit of the doubt.

Undoubtedly Jesus knew this and was preparing His followers for the challenges ahead when He spoke these encouraging words:

> Truly transformed are you who feel alienated in the cause of the Kingdom, because you recognize that the hope of heaven is yours for the asking.

> Truly transformed are you who grieve for a loved one lost, because you realize my Spirit longs to wrap His arms around you tonight.

> Truly transformed are you who seek to serve anyone whose need is greater than your own, because I, in turn, will meet your every need.

> Truly transformed are you whose spiritual appetite supersedes your physical desires, because my banquet table is full and I'm holding a chair for you.

> Truly transformed are you who forgive and forget, whose humility refuses to judge, because that will allow Me one day to treat you likewise.

Truly transformed are you when your heart invades My great heart, because only then will your mirror begin to reflect My image.

Truly transformed are you who resolve conflict even if it means a painful compromise, because as a result, all who surround you will seek to follow you anywhere.

Truly transformed are you when being My disciple begins to discipline you, because only then can the mature you start to see life's journey through a telescope.

Truly transformed are you when you become the target of lies and rumors simply for following in My footsteps, because you cannot believe the nice things I have said about you here in heaven—just like I said about Moses and Jonah and Daniel (Matt. 5:3-11, paraphrased by Jim Wilcox).

Notes

Chapter 1

1. Ray Bradbury, *Fahrenheit 451* (New York: Ballantine Books, 1979), 63.

Chapter 2

1. Quoted in Laura Sessions Stepp, "When We Race Through Life, We Miss It," *Dallas Morning News* (23 May 2000), 5C.

2. Ibid.

3. Michele McCormick, "We're Too Busy for Ideas," *Newsweek* (29 March 1993), 10.

4. Abraham McLaughlin, "Family Dinners Provide Food for Thought as Well," *Christian Science Monitor* (14 March 1996), 1.

5. Quoted in "Families That Eat Together," *Tufts University Health and Nutrition Letter* (October 1997), 2.

6. John J. Macionis, *Sociology,* 7th ed. (Upper Saddle River, N.J.: Prentice Hall), 108-10.

7. Tony Campolo, *Who Switched the Price Tags?* (Waco, Tex.: Word Books, 1986), 28-30.

8. Quoted in Stepp, "When We Race Through Life, We Miss It," 5C.

Chapter 3

1. Lisa Ko, "Technology Bogeymen!" *Yahoo Internet Life* (July 2000), 103.

2. Jean Nash Johnson, "CLICKS/Software Reviews," *Dallas Morning News* (3 August 2000), 3F.

3. Quoted in Austin Bunn, "Internet Madness," *Yahoo Internet Life* (July 2000), 100-103.

4. Ibid.

5. Ibid.

6. Ibid.

Chapter 4

1. Quoted in Miriam J. Hall, "Do Kids Count Where It Counts?" *Herald of Holiness* (June 1990), 20-23, 28.

2. Colin Powell, "Make a Promise to America's Children," *Parade Magazine* (24 December 2000), 4-5.

3. Quoted in Hall, "Do Kids Count Where It Counts?" 20-23, 28.

Chapter 5

1. Macionis, *Sociology*, 4-5.

2. Robert D. Putnam, "Bowling Alone: America's Declining Social Capital," *Journal of Democracy* 6 (1995): 65-78.

Chapter 6

1. John Stewart, *Bridges, Not Walls: A Book About Interpersonal Communication* (New York: Random House, 1986), 18-30.

Chapter 7

1. Sam Brody, "We Have Lost Our Humanity," *Newsweek* (7 September 1992), 8.

2. Michael R. Leming and George E. Dickinson, *Understanding Dying, Death, and Bereavement* (New York: Harcourt-Brace, 1998), 278-79.

3. Ibid., 15-17.

Chapter 8

1. Stephanie Coontz, *The Way We Never Were* (New York: Random House, 1994), 1-7.

2. Ibid., 1-2.

3. Arlene S. Skolnick and Jerome H. Skolnick, eds., *Family in Transition* (New York: Longman, 1997), 9.

Chapter 9

1. Reuben Welch, *We Really Do Need Each Other* (Nashville: Impact Books, 1973), 110.

2. Bob Benson, *Come Share the Being* (Brentwood, Tenn.: Solitude Celebration Press, 1974), 105.

Chapter 10

1. Barry Glassner, *The Culture of Fear: Why Americans Are Afraid of the Wrong Things* (New York: Basic Books, 1999), 1.

For Further Reading

Bane, M. J. *Here to Stay*. New York: Basic Books, 1976.

Bellah, Robert N., Robert Madsen, William M. Sullivan, Ann Swidler, and Steven M. Tipton Tipton. *The Good Society*. New York: Vintage, 1991.

———. *Habits of the Heart: Individualism and Community in American Life*. Berkeley and Los Angeles: University of California Press, 1985.

Benson, Bob. *Come Share the Being*. Brentwood, Tenn.: Solitude Celebration Press, 1974.

———. *In Quest of the Shared Life*. Nashville: Impact Books, 1981.

———. *Laughter in the Walls*. Nashville: Impact Books, 1969.

Berger, Peter, and R. Neuhaus. *To Empower People: The Role of Mediating Structures in Public Policy*. Washington, D.C.: American Enterprise Institute for Public Policy Research, 1977.

Bernard, Jesse. *The Sociology of Community*. Glenview, Ill.: Scott, Foresman, 1973.

Bradbury, Ray. *Fahrenheit 451*. New York: Ballantine Books, 1979.

Brody, Sam. "We Have Lost Our Humanity." *Newsweek*, 7 September 1992, 8.

Campolo, Tony. *Who Switched the Price Tags?* Waco, Tex.: Word Books, 1986.

Coles, Robert. *The Call of Service*. New York: Houghton-Mifflin, 1993.

Cooley, Charles Horton. *Social Organization: A Study of the Larger Mind*. New York: Charles Scribner's Sons, 1929.

Coontz, Stephanie. *The Way We Never Were*. New York: Random House, 1994.

Eldredge, John. *The Journey of Desire: Searching for the Life We've Only Dreamed Of*. Nashville: Thomas Nelson, 2000.

Eldredge, John, and Brent Curtis. *The Sacred Romance: Drawing Closer to the Heart of God*. Nashville: Thomas Nelson, 2001.

Etzioni, Amitai. *Rights and the Common Good: The Communitarian Perspective*. New York: St. Martin's Press, 1995.

———. *The Spirit of Community*. New York: Touchstone, 1993.

Ford, David. F. *The Shape of Living*. Grand Rapids: Baker Book House, 1997.

Fowler, Robert Booth. *The Dance with Community*. Lawrence, Kans.: University of Kansas Press, 1991.

Freie, John F. *Counterfeit Community: The Exploitation of Our Longings for Connectedness*. New York: Rowman and Littlefield, 1998.

Frohnen, Bruce. *The New Communitarians and the Crisis of Modern Liberalism*. Lawrence, Kans.: University of Kansas Press, 1996.

Gilligan, Carol. *In a Different Voice*. Cambridge, Mass.: Harvard University Press, 1982.

Gray, John. *Men Are from Mars, Women Are from Venus*. New York: HarperCollins, 1992.

Illich, Ivan. *Medical Nemesis*. New York: Pantheon Press, 1976.

Jameson, Frederic. "Postmodernism, or the Cultural Logic of Late Capitalism." *New Left Review* 146 (1984): 53-92.

Kretzmann, John P., and John L. McKnight. *Building Communities from the Inside Out: A Path Toward Finding and Mobilizing a Community's Assets*. Chicago: ACTA Publications, 1993.

Langdon, Philip. *A Better Place to Live*. New York: Harper-Collins, 1994.

Lasch, Christopher. *Haven in a Heartless World*. New York: Basic Books, 1977.

Lucado, Max. *In the Grip of Grace*. Waco, Tex.: Word Books, 1996.

Manning, Brennan. *Abba's Child: The Cry of the Heart for Intimate Belonging*. Colorado Springs: Navpress, 1994.

————. *The Signature of Jesus: On the Pages of Our Lives.* Portland, Oreg.: Multnomah Press, 1992.

Manning, Doug. *Don't Take My Grief Away.* New York: Harper-Collins, 1984.

Marty, Martin E. *The One and the Many.* Cambridge, Mass.: Harvard University Press, 1997.

Mattessich, Paul, and Barbara Monsey. *Community Building: What Makes It Work: A Review of Factors Influencing Successful Community Building.* St. Paul, Minn.: Amherst H. Wilder Foundation, 1997.

McKnight, John. *The Careless Society.* New York: Basic Books, 1995.

McMinn, Mark, and James Foster. *Christians in the Crossfire.* Newberg, Oreg.: Barclay, 1990.

Medoff, Peter, and Holly Sklar. *Streets of Hope: The Fall and Rise of an Urban Neighborhood.* Cambridge, Mass.: South End Press, 1994.

Merelman, Richard. M. *Making Something of Ourselves: Our Culture and Politics in the United States.* Berkeley, Calif.: University of California Press, 1984.

Myrdal, Gunnar. *An American Dilemma: The Negro Problem and Modern Democracy.* New York: Harper and Row, 1944.

Naisbitt, John. *Megatrends.* New York: Warner Books, 1982.

Nouen, Henri J. M., Donald P. McNeill, and Douglas A. Morrison. *Compassion: A Reflection on the Christian Life.* New York: Image Books, 1982.

Palmer, Parker. *The Courage to Teach.* San Francisco: Jossey-Bass, 1998.

Pipher, Mary. *The Shelter of Each Other.* New York: Ballentine Books, 1996.

Price, Sharon J., Patrick C. McKenry, and Megan J. Murphy, eds. *Families Across Time.* Los Angeles: Roxbury, 2000.

Putnam, Robert D. "Bowling Alone: America's Declining Social Capital." *Journal of Democracy* 6 (1995): 65-78.

Rheingold, Howard. *The Virtual Community: Homesteading on the Electronic Frontier.* New York: HarperPerennial, 1993.

Rubin, Lillian. *Families on the Fault Line: America's Working Class Speaks About the Family, Economy, Race and Ethnicity.* New York: Harper Collins, 1995.

Schorr, Lisbeth B. *Common Purpose: Strenthening Families and Neighborhoods to Rebuild America.* New York: Anchor Books, 1997.

————. *Within Our Reach.* New York: Doubleday, 1989.

Sider, Ronald J. *Just Generosity.* Grand Rapids: Baker Books, 1999.

————. *Rich Christians in an Age of Hunger.* Dallas: Word Books, 1997.

Simon, David, and Edward Burns. *The Corner: A Year in the Life of an Inner-City Neighborhood.* New York: Broadway Books, 1997.

Sine, Tom. *Mustard Seed Versus McWorld.* Grand Rapids: Baker Books, 1999.

Skolnick, Arlene S., and Jerome H. Skolnick, eds. *Family in Transition.* New York: Longman, 1997.

Sweet, Leonard. *Eleven Genetic Gateways to Spiritual Awakening.* Nashville: Abingdon Press, 1998.

————. *SoulTsunami: Sink or Swim in New Millennium Culture.* Grand Rapids: Zondervan Publishing House, 1999.

Taylor, Ella. *Prime Time Families.* Berkeley, Calif.: University of California Press, 1989.

Thompson, David L. *Holiness for Hurting People.* Indianapolis: Wesleyan Publishing House, 1998.

Wallis, Jim. *The Soul of Politics.* San Diego: Harcourt Brace, 1995.

Welch, Rueben. *We Really Do Need Each Other.* Nashville: Impact Books, 1973.

Willimon, William H., and Thomas H. Naylor. *The Abandoned Generation.* Grand Rapids: William B. Eerdmans Publishing Co., 1995.